LOW
CARB
IS
LEKKER
Two

INÈ REYNIERSE

Author's Acknowledgements

To my family, you are my 'happy place'. There is so much greatness evident in you guys – I'd better feed you well! Always.

To my home-base team, Sumaya Jacobs, Filander de Bruin (Fiela) and Evanjholene Ross (Wennie) – you were such a big part of the miracle of this book. Thanks for being my hands when mine were simply not enough. Sumaya, you are a truly talented chef in the making.

To each and every 'Low Carbie' and every Facebook page friend – I thought of you during the late-night recipe testing sessions. Your kind comments and sincere feedback inspired me to keep finding better and tastier ways to 'decarb' those all-time favourites we used to love.

To my production team – you guys are all masters of your trades. (I'll be the judge!) It was simply a marvellous privilege to work with the same team on this book.

A special thanks to The Garden Shed guesthouse and Au' de Hex Boutique Hotel in Wellington for allowing us to shoot and stay at your immaculate venues.

Last, but definitely not least, I have been on the receiving end of abundant and truly AMAZING GRACE throughout this project. My heart fully and undeniably resonates with Psalm 8!

Published by Struik Lifestyle
(an imprint of Penguin Random House South Africa (Pty) Ltd)
Reg. No. 1953/000441/07
The Estuaries, 4 Oxbow Crescent, Century Avenue, Century City, 7441
PO Box 1144, Cape Town, 8000 South Africa

Visit www.penguinrandomhouse.co.za for updates, news, events and special offers.

First published in 2017

Publisher: Linda de Villiers
Managing editor: Cecilia Barfield
Editor and indexer: Joy Clack
Designer: Beverley Dodd
Proofreader: Glynne Newlands
Photographer: Sean Calitz
Food stylist: Brita du Plessis
Food stylist's assistant: Elizabeth Ingram
Food preparation: Elizabeth Ingram and Sumaya Jacobs

Reproduction by Hirt & Carter Cape (Pty) Ltd
Printed and bound by CTP Printers, Duminy Street, Parow, 7500, South Africa

ISBN: 978 1 43230 688 5

Contents

Forewords

I spend a lot of my time sorting out people's hormones. No, I am not an endocrinologist. I am a sexologist (of all things!) and a medical doctor.

Many of my patients suffer from hormonal imbalances. Their individual hormones might fall in 'normal' reference ranges, but the ratios are out, wreaking havoc with their sex lives, weight, mood, fertility and general wellbeing. Many have been told that 'everything is normal' and that 'it is all in your head', leaving them frustrated, desperate and unwell.

The reality is that sorting out a person's hormones is not as easy as throwing tablets at them. But, it is not that complicated either. It is about getting the basics right. Sleep. Exercise. Play. Eat clean.

Eating clean sounds boring and like an insurmountable task, until you read Inè's practical suggestions and try out her easy, tasty recipes. I am speaking for many of my patients, my family, the friends who eat at our house and certainly Annah, who prepares our food, when I am saying that I am thoroughly looking forward to all the healthy yumminess that is to come from this latest version of *Low Carb is Lekker*!

DR ELNA RUDOLPH
(Clinical Head of My Sexual Health, a multidisciplinary team of sexual healthcare providers in Johannesburg, Pretoria, Witbank and Cape Town.)

Leading medical research organisations recognise that the main non-infectious diseases plaguing modern societies are heart disease, diabetes and stroke. They generally agree that all of these diseases are linked to a disorder of carbohydrate metabolism.

The regrettable prevalence of these diseases in modern societies is thought to be linked largely to diet. Advances in genetic research illustrate that we are individually diverse, and no single guideline will work for everybody. This has been borne out by research as well as the health benefits experienced by many people who have experimented successfully with low-carbohydrate diets.

The nutritional community is currently highly polarised between those clinging to a paradigm that has clearly not served a significant segment of the population, and anti-carbohydrate activists who are revolutionary and zealous campaigners. Inè is a breath of fresh air. I trust that her book will convey her good-natured sincerity and offer delicious, practical dishes to people who may benefit from low-carb eating.

RAEL KOPING R.D.

From the author

'Why are you following a low-carb lifestyle and what is keeping you from eating a hamburger and fries as we speak?'

I asked this random question on my Facebook page one evening. I hit 'post', my heart racing …

I was terrified to read the responses. I was so scared I would read comments like 'I want to lose weight!'. Now don't get me wrong here – there's

nothing wrong with losing weight. I'm all for it, in fact. But … if I squeezed my last ounce of energy into a process simply to help someone to drop a dress size or to fit into a new pair of designer jeans … *eish*.

Aside: This was all taking place during a very intense time of my life. A time where stopping for take-aways after a crazy day would have made a really big difference for me. My twin girls had just started walking (in opposite directions mostly), I had

had a year of very little sleep, a book that launched and took on a life of its own, two coming-of-age teens (a daughter who was deputy head girl at her school, and a son who I was homeschooling), a husband with his own gas business during a countrywide gas crisis, a new product line, TWINS, food demonstrations and a looming deadline for the next book, which meant several hours in my kitchen testing and thinking of creative new recipes – all during a Wellington heat wave that lasted for two months straight. Oh, and did I mention twins?

Back to my story … The responses started rolling in one after the other:
- Insulin resistance under control; weight came off.
- Diabetic – glucose levels optimal – EVERYTHING WORKS BETTER, lost weight, off CPAP.
- Acne is so much better.
- As a family we love it! No cravings, just a way of life.
- It worked for my eczema. Brings down blood pressure. Our family no longer takes meds for Type 2 diabetes, migraines, ADHD, depression, anxiety, asthma, eczema, psoriasis and arthiritis.
- Child on the autism spectrum improved so much.
- first time something that worked and I experienced weight loss. Helped with bloating.
- Helped with epileptic seizures.
- Postnatal depression and Hashimoto's disease under control.
- No more IBS.

It went on and on… I was already holding back the tears when this response came in: 'The concept of sugar feeding cancer made sense and I wanted to give myself every opportunity to beat the bastard!' I knew the weight of this statement too well. You only have to see someone you love go through this devastation once.

I got up from behind my computer with an indescribable sense of thankfulness. Real people with real struggles found REAL results. And losing weight for most was a real added bonus.

Many explained and described what I had discovered along with my family a few years before – a health-boosting lifestyle with the potential to restore, replenish, reshape, re-energise as well as reduce and reverse. This was NOT just another diet.

For many, this precious little penny has dropped and became a priceless, quality of life investment, for themselves and the ones they love.

It's been four and a half years and counting since my last commercial doughnut, milkshake, muffin, pizza, toast, pretzels, cookies, hamburger or chips.
- Do I miss them? Nope.
- Do I feel deprived? Nope.
- Do I need to be so strict? Probably not, but if I don't miss it or feel deprived by the absence of it, it indicates that I am enjoying life's tastes and textures.

It really is something you cannot explain to someone until they experience it for themselves.

I practise mindful eating habits in order to keep my blood sugar levels in check so that I can have a stable mood and a constant source of energy without being ruled by cravings day in and out.

I AM NOT ON A DIET

Sadly, we have gone from a time where our normal food preferences or staples were referred to as our 'diet' to a time where the word 'diet' has become a profit-turning term for a specific formula with the sole purpose to restrict and deprive. And because banking on willpower is not a very sustainable system for us humans, 'miracle' weight-loss products were invented to side step the willpower element altogether. So most diets are simply a setup for failure, relying on willpower in the midst of hunger and cravings, without teaching us to be responsible stewards of the foods we allow to enter our bodies.

I AM NOT ON A DIET. I AM ON A MINDFUL EATING MISSION!

DISCLAIMER: I am not a health professional. Always speak to a health professional before making lifestyle/health changes. This is what worked for me and my family and others who shared experiences with me. My main aim is to share recipes and some concepts that clarified this journey for us.

A matter of principles

A QUICK BUT SURREAL TRUE STORY...

My husband, Louis, decided to start strength training after following the LCHF lifestyle for a little over a year and a half. He felt energised and wanted to put this newfound energy to good use after many years of being too tired, sick and overweight.

So, like all things he does, he jumped in with enthusiasm and commitment and came home telling me about some of the interesting conversations he had. This one in particular stood out for me:

An older guy came up to Louis and, knowing his lifestyle preference, he told Louis that he had also followed a LCHF 'diet' for a while with amazing results. He even lost about 10 kg and felt great until he ate regular wheat bread again. He went on to explain that when he ate the bread and felt so sick afterwards, he decided it wasn't worth following LCHF if it was going to make him ill. Instead of seeking to understand the way his body reacted when he reintroduced bread into his diet, he instead blamed the lifestyle for exposing the truth about his body's real reaction to wheat, thus spoiling his bread-loving fun. Something he was not prepared to give up.

PRINCIPLE ONE

If it's a lifestyle and not a diet, you are doing what you believe is BEST for you and your health in the long term.

Leaving the back door open to a processed and artificial food lifestyle means this is simply an attempt to quickly treat some symptoms (be it weight gain or poor health) without committing long term to change the root of the problem.

Committing to the root means that you're in it to win it – through every season life throws at you. It means you are raising the bar with your food choices and not compromising with nutritionally second-best food sources.

So, will the occasional slice of white bread or Peppermint Crisp tart kill you? Absolutely not! As long as you know you are settling for second best when you do choose to eat processed, sugar-laden foods and not the other way around.

In my opinion, the 'everything in moderation' way of thinking is critically misleading, giving many a false sense of wellbeing. What does 'everything in moderation' actually mean? Is it eating equal amounts of everything healthy and unhealthy, as long as you eat some healthy? Is it living a little and

eating whatever you feel like today, and then drinking water and veggie juice tomorrow to cancel out the impact of today's food? Or is it the one I hear most often: 'Surely, a little [*fill in the blank*] won't hurt, will it?'

If everyday food choices become a constant negotiation between the healthy and unhealthy kinds of food we are going to eat in moderation, what does a lifetime of moderation look like in the end? Do we only get moderately ill from the diseases it brings?

If it is a lifestyle and not simply a diet, you will accept the fact that your biochemistry is as unique as the prints on your fingers and what works for others, might not work for you. You could handle more or fewer carbs than the next person. Being healthy, energy filled and craving free is the goal here. That is the balance that you need to find for yourself. Also, being the weight your frame was designed to carry for the work it was meant to do should be what you are content with – nothing more, nothing less.

WHAT MOST DIETS REALLY DO

Your body has a happy place or 'set point'. It is the place on the scale or the clothing size that your body maintains as a safe point to sustain you through abundance and scarcity. This is the gist in layman's terms. I can, however, recommend Jonathan Bailor's book, *The Calorie Myth*, for those who need the scientific terminologies and official medical papers to support the science.

Usually your body will allow your weight to move within about 10% left and right on the scale and metabolically adjust all systems from there before what people would describe as a plateau happens. For example, if someone weighs 65 kg, their set point could easily move between 58.5 kg and 71.5 kg. Problem is, once you have one Christmas of 'moderate' feasting on cookies, ice cream, pudding and chocolate, your new set point may be 68 kg, making your body's new happy place anywhere from 62 kg to 75 kg. Now your ideal weight of 58 kg suddenly falls into a different bracket altogether and it is usually during this realisation that drastic measures are implemented.

Bring on the [*fill in the blank*] diet – your punishment for 'living' in the moment – only to find out that your best efforts are not moving the scale and you are certain the universe is against you.

I'm referring to that irritating crash diet phenomenon you might have experienced that causes you to lose only 125.568 grams after jogging for hours while drinking the juice of half a carrot and eating a quarter of a bleak-looking rice cake. Then, after being 'good', you celebrate life's small victories and you allow yourself two-and-a-half licks of ice cream, just to find yourself weighing 1.25 kg more than before the bleak rice cake regime took over. Why is this?

The answer is that your body decided to slow down your metabolism because there was obviously a huge worldwide famine going on and just in case things take a turn for the worse, it decided to store the first available foods as fat.

This is why yo-yo dieting causes so much damage in the long run.

A happy body is a body that can be fed thin. (Now there's a mind shift.) In a place of real-food nutritional abundance there is no need for the body to compromise metabolism or for hormones to be placed on full alert to possibly enter fight or flight mode in case of a life-threatening starvation. The problem is, the body never forgets. It doesn't forget the periods you denied it food. It doesn't forget the way you punished yourself for the binge eating. Our bodies need us to be our own best friend again before it will simply give away the one thing it was programmed to do – help us survive as long as possible in the face of danger or famine by holding on and building our fat stores.

PRINCIPLE TWO

**If it's a lifestyle and not a diet, you can and should stop starving yourself.
Your body was wired to fight for you to survive. Reward your body with the best
possible nutrition to let it thrive and not just survive.**

Rather feed your body thin with enough clean nutrients to keep your metabolism and hormones happy and working to your advantage.

1. Eat plenty of clean carbs! Yes, you heard me. It's called low carb, not NO carb. No carbs mean NO nutrient-dense balance between soluble and insoluble fibre and that is NOT a smart move as far as I'm concerned.
2. If you are trying to beat obesity or fighting back against diabetes, stick to nutrient-dense non-starchy veggies in abundance and lower carb fruit and veggies (berries, pumpkin, marrows, tomatoes etc.) in moderation. If you and your family are healthy and just find it liberating to be eating real food, enjoy a variety of real food! (You can even enjoy the OCCASIONAL starchy veggie within the right ratio, cooked in healthy fats. You settled into LCHF lifestyle mode ... now LIVE!) Part of the beauty of a lifestyle is the fact that you maintain weight, health and healthy metabolism within the some higher carb and some lower carb days that normal life brings. As long as you get to know your happy carb range, where you don't experience sudden cravings and maintain a healthy body fat for your age. Keep the grain- free, sugar-free, unprocessed food basics in check and the rest will fall into place.
3. Eat clean, hormone- and antibiotic-free fats and clean (in other words, grass-fed and free-range, preferably organic if you can get it) sources of protein to keep your metabolism and endocrine systems working healthily in your favour.

PRINCIPLE THREE

**If it's a lifestyle and not a diet, the quality of the fat and protein-rich foods you consume
is of the HIGHEST importance.**

Doing a crash one-month LCHF diet to lose a few kilos for that important function is one thing. Choosing LCHF as a lifestyle changes the stakes completely.

More than ever, the source of the fat you consume needs to make sense too. With all the growth hormones, antibiotics, GMOs and pesticides in the foods being fed to commercially raised animals, there can be no pride in eating a steak with its fat on or that crunchy pork belly. The problem is that these animals mainly store all these toxins in their fat, which is what LCHF now prioritises as our main source of energy. These toxin-filled fats are also high-oestrogen foods that can be very harmful to your health by destroying your hormone balance and, according to several health experts, can lead to health issues such as hypothyroidism, autoimmune disease, chronic fatigue and ovarian cancer. The best way to beat the toxins and avoid all the excess oestrogens is to gradually budget and switch over to the following:

- Grass-fed beef and the butter from these healthy animals.
- Free-range lamb, pork, chicken and eggs.
- Hormone-, antibiotic- and GMO-free full-cream milk, cream, amasi and double-cream plain yoghurt (such as Fair Cape's product range).

It's been almost three years since we last bought our meat from a general grocer. Today, we are a few families who buy bulk grass-fed beef, acorn-fed pork and Karoo lamb together and we save at least a third to a half of the store-priced products. We can barely eat storebought meat anymore – there is a huge difference in taste once you get used to the real deal again.

And while we are on the topic, flavour your clean proteins with Himalayan or sea salt, MSG-free and non-irradiated spices and the occasional GMO-free soy sauce (I use Bragg's liquid aminos, available from Dis-Chem and health stores). These are good 'clean food' products to incorporate into your daily meal preparations.

MORE HEALTHY FATS
- Avocado
- Avocado oil
- Fatty fish
- Coconut
- Coconut oil
- Extra virgin olive oil
- Butter from grass-fed cows
- Free-range eggs
- Dark chocolate (not in bulk and not daily, ladies)
- Cheese and high-fat GMO- and hormone-free dairy products (if you are not dairy intolerant)
- Chia seeds
- Rendered fats from grass-fed and/or free-range animals

So, what does healthy fat look like on a plate? Do I simply swap my bowl of pasta for a bowl of butter? What does a 'high' amount of fat look like?

Let me explain. Energy from food is measured in kilojoules (kJ), which is an easy way to get a glimpse at how much each type of food will fuel you (or what gives you more bang for your buck, so to speak).

Energy breakdown
- 1 gram of protein = 17 kJ
- 1 gram of carbohydrates = 17 kJ
- 1 gram of dietary fibre = 8 kJ
- 1 gram of alcohol = 29 kJ
- 1 gram of fat = 37 kJ

As you can see, fat will fuel you for longer and a little bit sure goes a long way.

The current WESTERN DIET recommendation is to eat:
- 30% lean protein
- 20% fat (mostly unsaturated)
- 50% carbohydrates (mostly from grains, legumes, starches and sugar).

An average LCHF lifestyle would consist of:
- 25% CLEAN protein (hormone-, antibiotic- and GMO-feed free)
- 15% CLEAN mostly non-starchy carbohydrates, moderate starchy veg and high-fibre, lower carb fruit such as berries
- 60% HEALTHY fats.

Within these ratios some people might stay in ketosis*, while others might have to drop carbs a bit and add to fats if ketosis is needed for a medical condition or preference. The bottom line is that you're in it to win it, right? Therefore, I would rather opt for a slightly higher amount of carbs and a lifetime of sustainable benefits. Even the experts are all over the show when it comes to the perfect macro nutrient ratios. The key is to find harmony between satiety and energy without any sign of cravings. Simply put, you want to achieve nutritional 'happiness' instead of 'hangriness'. Being tired, hungry, angry and craving-driven means you need to adjust your macro ratios a bit.

* Ketosis is an extremely high fat-burning state that the body enters into upon restricting carb or sugar intake. During ketosis the brain runs on fat, via ketone bodies. These are energy molecules in the blood, much like blood sugar, and can become fuel for our brains via conversion from fat by the liver.

Hypothetically, for a woman (age 18–50) trying to lose weight, this will mean roughly 6 400 kJ a day broken down as follows:

- 3 840 kJ from healthy fats (to achieve this, you need to eat 103 g fat)
- 1 600 kJ from protein (to achieve this, you need to eat 94 g protein)
- 960 kJ from carbohydrates (you can eat up to 56 g of clean carbs).

Keep in mind you are completely unique in bio-chemistry, activity level etc. This serves as a generic example only.

As I have said before, with fats a little goes a very long way. To give you an idea:
1 serving (±30 g) healthy fat equals:
- 2 Tbsp coconut oil, olive oil, avocado oil or butter
- 4 Tbsp chia seeds, or nuts and seeds.

When we cook, this is the amount of healthy fat (in the form of oil) we mostly use when sautéing or frying. If you can include this into your three meals, a snack and/or a smoothie, you have 100–120 g of healthy fats already. This is not even counting the 8.5 g of fat in a cup of milk you use for coffee during the day, the 10 g of fat in 30 g of cheese, the 11.2 g fat in 2 Tbsp fresh cream or the 10 g of fat in two large eggs. And then there are the fatty, free-range or grass-fed meats that also bring extremely healthy sources of fat to the table.

PRINCIPLE FOUR

If it's a lifestyle and not a diet, be balanced within the bigger picture.

Do not underestimate what stress and lack of sleep can do to your hormones. I have seen for myself that even when you eat all the right foods, if your hormones are unhappy, chances are they will hold on to fat or, worse, keep storing fat.

GREAT STRATEGIES FOR HEALTHY HORMONES:

- Try to eat enough fibre daily to get rid of excess toxins or oestrogens.
- Eat and prioritise good sources of omega-3, such as fatty fish and grass-fed protein sources.
- Try to sleep for at least eight hours a night.
- Combat stress effects on your hormones by starting a high-intensity interval training or a weight training programme two to three times a week. It is a great way to boost metabolism and reset your healthy hormone balance.
- According to Dr Alan Christianson, higher carb meals (± 20 g) should be avoided early in your day and rather eaten in the evenings. In his book, *The Adrenal Reset Diet*, he explains strategies that can help restore natural cortisol rhythms.
- Avoid BPA plastics and Teflon pans and eliminate as many toxins from your daily foods as you can. Read labels, avoid GMO- and hormone-filled meats. Rather avoid animal fats if you cannot find grass-fed sources and focus on clean fats such as avocados, olive oil etc. Add maca powder to your smoothie in the morning as a hormonal tonic.

According to Dr Sara Gottfried, author of *The Hormone Reset Diet*, you could benefit from a lower range low-carb lifestyle if:

- you have polycystic ovarian syndrome (PCOS);
- you eat a lot of carbs (greater than 250 g daily);
- you have been unable to lose weight; or
- you are diabetic (type 1 or type 2).

However, if you have been struggling with your thyroid, going too low carb (less than 50 g a day) could have a negative impact on your health.

Unless it is a medical necessity, it is not recommended going too low carb (less than 30 g a day) for too long, for most women.

Find your low carb 'happy place' – the place where you thrive with enough energy and a healthy immune system. This is different for everybody.

The carb counts of some of my meals are intentionally a bit higher to help you find your feet within a lower carb, long-term lifestyle. The basics are still the same: eat when you are hungry and stop when you are full.

LCHF = Low Carb Healthy Fat

In my experience it is easier to focus on LCHF as Low Carb Healthy Fat. I found the 'high' of 'high fat' very confusing, especially when it came to portions. What is funny, though, is that I ate way more fats (mostly unhealthy) during my fat phobic years than I do now. See the healthy fats list and portion sizes on p. 9.

LCHF = Low Carb Healthy Fibre

Fibre is a valuable part of a low-carb lifestyle. It can keep blood sugar regulated and can also help the body get rid of toxins, especially excess oestrogen. Fibre also aids satiety and is great for creating a healthy gut environment. It is important to note that people with certain conditions should not consume too much fibre. Experts advise to gradually work your way up to a higher fibre intake for best results.

LCHF = Low Carb Healthy Freakin' hormones

Many health professionals devote a lifetime to understanding the complexities of the endocrine system. (The struggle is real, ladies!) It is important, however, to keep a balanced LCHF lifestyle approach between allowing hormones to heal – consuming real, unprocessed, sugar-free foods and healthy fats – and then ensuring they stay healthy via making good lifestyle choices.

Dough you still love me?

I AM SO EXCITED TO SHARE MY NEW DOUGH RECIPES AND *ALL* THEIR VARIATIONS WITH YOU. DOUGHS 1 TO 4 ARE VERY EASY TO MAKE, BUT USE A SLIGHTLY UNCONVENTIONAL TECHNIQUE THAT I PERFECTED OVER WHAT FELT LIKE 10 000 HOURS! (I CONFESS THAT EVERY TIME I 'DECARB' A COMFORT FOOD USING THIS DOUGH CONCEPT, I UNASHAMEDLY DO A HAPPY DANCE.) DOUGHS 5 TO 7 ARE MORE FAMILIAR IN METHOD AND YOU SHOULD BE ABLE TO EASILY FIND YOUR WAY AROUND THEM. DOUGH 8 IS A VARIATION ON DOUGHS 1 TO 4, USING AN EGG REPLACEMENT. I PUT IT IN LAST SIMPLY BECAUSE IT IS SLIGHTLY HIGHER IN CARBS, WHICH KIDS CAN HANDLE, BUT ADULTS CAN ENJOY IT OCCASIONALLY AS AN ALLERGEN-FREE OPTION. I KNOW HOW DESPERATELY WE TRY TO BE HEALTHY YET RETAIN A SENSE OF 'NORMAL'. THE TECHNIQUE I USE YIELDS A DOUGH THAT RESEMBLES A GLUTEN-LIKE DOUGH BALL – MY LITTLE GIFT OF 'NORMAL' TO ALL THE LOVELY INDIVIDUALS AND FAMILIES FOLLOWING A LOW-CARB LIFESTYLE.

New to the baking team

I HAVE INCORPORATED SOME NEW STAPLES IN MY LIST OF INGREDIENTS. I STILL MAKE USE OF NUT FLOURS, BUT MY FOCUS FOR THIS BOOK IS BUDGET FRIENDLY, ALLERGY FRIENDLY AND ACCESSIBILITY. DOUGHS 1, 2 AND 3 CAN BE MADE WITH A FEW FLOUR VARIATIONS, SO UNLESS A RECIPE CALLS FOR A SPECIFIC COMBINATION, YOU CAN USE WHATEVER IS AVAILABLE.

SUNFLOWER SEED FLOUR

You can buy this from online stores and select suppliers (visit www.lowcarbislekker.co.za for details), or you can grind your own in a coffee grinder. Remember, the finer the flour the better the batter. In my experience, the storebought flour works like a charm every time.

Sunflower seed flour is packed with vitamin E. Sunflower seeds are one of the finest sources of B-complex vitamins, and they are also an incredibly rich source of many essential minerals, including calcium, iron, manganese, zinc, magnesium, selenium and copper.

Sunflower seed flour is, however, slightly higher in carbs than nut flours, which is not a problem if you are doing a lower carb, family lifestyle approach or even if you are planning on just eating budget dough-based recipes once in a while. It should NOT cause a sugar spike if eaten within the suggested portion guidelines.

This flour is also a welcome option for people or kids with nut allergies and I personally found it to be very baby-first-food friendly.

For a lower carb option, replace 1 cup of sunflower seed flour with 1 cup of macadamia or almond flour. Pecan flour does not work as well for these dough recipes.

COCONUT FLOUR

Storebought works best for doughs 4 and 5.

GOLDEN FLAX MEAL

Dough 2 uses golden flax meal along with sunflower seed flour, which puts it in a lower carb bracket. (Brown flax meal will work too, but it has a stronger flavour.) The flax is needed for the right consistency of the nachos and tacos, but can be replaced with nut or sunflower seed flour for the flammkuchen and quesadilla. Available from online stores and select suppliers (visit www.lowcarbislekker.co.za for details).

CHIA SEEDS

They can be a bit pricey but, trust me, a little bit goes a very long way! You will need a coffee grinder to grind them for these recipes. After the first batch, you will simply fall in love with them. They are available at supermarkets and health stores.

GELATINE POWDER

A gut-healing super food that we seldom get enough of in our diet. It is also an excellent source of protein, and wonderful for your skin, hair, nails and joints. For vegetarians and vegans, agar-agar can be used instead of gelatine in the recipes; however, it does not provide the same protein as gelatine.

DOUGH 1

USE THIS DOUGH FOR: FLATBREAD, HERBED FLATBREAD, STUFFED BUNS, SAUSAGE ROLLS, CHEESE STRAWS, SAVOURY BAGELS, PIZZA (REGULAR THIN BASE), CRACKERS, MINI HAMBURGER BUNS, MEAT PIES AND BREAD.

RECIPE	PORTIONS	TOTAL CARBS	FIBRE	NET CARBS	FAT	PROTEIN	KJ
Dough 1	Entire batch; made with 2 cups sunflower seed flour	54.8 g	36.8 g	18 g	123.8 g	45.1 g	5 644
Dough 1	4; made with 2 cups sunflower seed flour	13.5 g	9.2 g	4.3 g	26.3 g	7.8 g	1 238
Dough 1	Entire batch; made with 1 cup sunflower seed flour + 1 cup nut flour	51.6 g	35.9 g	15.7 g	114.1 g	41.4 g	5 212
Dough 1	Entire batch; made with 2 cups nut flour	48.4 g	34.9 g	13.5 g	104.4 g	38 g	4 776

¾ cup water
60 g butter
2 cups sunflower seed flour (alternatively, you can use 1 cup sunflower seed flour and 1 cup nut flour of choice)
1 tsp salt
1 tsp paprika
1 Tbsp psyllium husk powder
2 eggs
½ cup grated cheese (optional for sausage rolls, meat pies, cheese straws and kiddie crackers)
¼ cup sunflower seed flour or nut flour for sprinkling and handling the dough

In a medium-sized, heavy-bottomed saucepan, warm the water and butter together on medium heat. You don't want the water to boil before the butter has melted properly, so take things nice and slow.

Mix the 2 cups flour, salt, paprika and psyllium husk powder in a separate bowl, making sure the psyllium is mixed in evenly.

As soon as the butter has melted and the water starts to boil, add the dry ingredients to the saucepan and stir until the mixture forms a ball of dough. Turn the heat to the lowest setting and cook the dough ball while moving it around in the saucepan for about 1 minute. You want the dough to have an elastic but firm-to-the-touch consistency.

Remove the saucepan from the heat and place the dough ball in a mixing bowl. Allow to cool for 5 minutes.

Now, break the eggs into the mixing bowl with the dough ball, add the grated cheese and mix with an electric beater for about 1 minute. Scrape all the dough from the sides and beat and work into a soft dough ball. Sprinkle with a little of the extra flour and use your hands to shape the dough into a non-sticky, slightly glossy ball for 10–20 seconds. This is literally just to shape the dough; don't try to knead it like you would with glutinous doughs.

Wrap the dough ball in plastic wrap and pop into the freezer for 5 minutes or into the refrigerator for up to three days. Then simply shape it and bake it according to your chosen recipe.

Pizza Base

PIZZA AND ITALY ARE PRETTY MUCH SYNONYMOUS TODAY. HOWEVER, PIZZA WAS INVENTED ONLY IN THE EARLY NINETEENTH CENTURY, WHEN IT WAS SERVED AS A HUMBLE STREET FOOD IN NAPLES. ITS POPULARITY SPREAD ABROAD AFTER A LOCAL PIZZA-MAKER DESIGNED A PIZZA IN HONOUR OF QUEEN MARGHERITA WHEN SHE VISITED NAPLES IN 1889. SHE WAS CHARMED BY THE PIZZA WITH THE COLOURS OF THE NEW FLAG OF THE JUST-UNIFIED ITALY – RED TOMATOES, WHITE MOZZARELLA AND GREEN BASIL. WHAT MAKES A PIZZA ABSOLUTELY IRRESISTIBLE IS GOOD QUALITY, FRESH INGREDIENTS AND A PIZZA OVEN. THE BASE PLAYS AN IMPORTANT ROLE TOO. I ALMOST GAVE UP ON DECARBING PIZZA ALTOGETHER UNTIL, THROUGH A SERIES OF PECULIAR EVENTS IN TRYING TO REMAKE ANOTHER RECIPE, THE PIZZA BASE WAS BORN. AND THE REST, AS THEY SAY, IS HISTORY!

RECIPE	PORTIONS	TOTAL CARBS	FIBRE	NET CARBS	FAT	PROTEIN	KJ
Pizza base	1 pizza	27 g	18.4 g	8.6 g	52.5 g	15.5 g	2 368

1 quantity Dough 1, without the cheese (opposite)

Preheat the oven to 180 °C.

Prepare the dough as described in the recipe, leaving out the cheese. Take the chilled dough ball and divide it into two equal parts. Using a rolling pin, roll each piece directly onto baking paper. Aim for a thickness of 3–5 mm. (Leave the bases on the baking paper until you are ready to serve.)

Bake for 10–15 minutes directly on the wire oven rack. The base should move easily on the baking paper, but shouldn't be crusty yet. Now you can go ahead and treat these babies to some delicious toppings of your choice and bake until the cheese is melted and bubbly and the base is nice and crusty. Or you can cool the bases, cover them in plastic wrap and freeze for later.

Yields 2 pizza bases
I would suggest half a pizza to be a good, filling portion.

LEKKER TIP

For a Margherita-style base, add some tomato paste, 1 tsp xylitol, fresh garlic, basil and mozzarella cheese.

QUICK COMPARISON FOR ONE MARGHERITA PIZZA:

Regular – about 160 g carbs per pizza

Gluten-free – 180 g carbs per pizza

My low-carb pizza base with Margherita-style toppings – less than 20 g carbs per pizza (and it tastes like REAL pizza!)

Basic dough bread

THIS BREAD IS SIMPLY LOVELY. IT IS SIMILAR TO A LIGHT RYE BREAD, BUT WITHOUT THE OVERPOWERING TASTE. THE BREAD HAS A DENSE BUT SOFT TEXTURE AND, IN MY OPINION, COMES INTO ITS OWN AFTER A DAY IN THE REFRIGERATOR.

RECIPE	PORTIONS	TOTAL CARBS	FIBRE	NET CARBS	FAT	PROTEIN	KJ
Basic bread	2-slice serving	8 g	4.4 g	3.6 g	30.6 g	9.6 g	1 324

2 quantities Dough 1, without cheese, but with an extra ½ tsp salt (p. 14)
1 egg for egg wash

Preheat the oven to 180 °C. Line a loaf pan with baking paper.

Prepare the dough as described in the recipe, leaving out the cheese and adding the extra salt to the batter. You don't need to chill this dough. Simply place into the prepared loaf pan, brush liberally with the egg wash and bake for 1 hour.

Remove the bread from the pan and allow to cool completely before slicing. This bread will keep well in an airtight container in the refrigerator for up to four days. It can also be thinly sliced, portioned and frozen for up to a month.

Yields 1 loaf at 25.1 g net carbs per loaf (12–16 slices)

DOUGH 2

THIS DOUGH IS CRISPIER THAN DOUGH 1. WHEN 1 CUP OF THE SUNFLOWER SEED FLOUR IS REPLACED WITH 1 CUP GOLDEN FLAX MEAL, IT BRINGS MEXICAN FAVOURITES LIKE NACHOS AND TACOS RIGHT TO YOUR DOORSTEP! USE THIS DOUGH FOR: FLAMMKUCHEN (PIZZA WITH A VERY THIN BASE), QUESADILLA, NACHOS AND TACOS.

RECIPE	PORTIONS	TOTAL CARBS	FIBRE	NET CARBS	FAT	PROTEIN	KJ
Dough 2	Entire batch; made with 2 cups sunflower seed flour	54.8 g	36 g	18.8 g	100.4 g	25.2 g	4 684
Dough 2	4; made with 2 cups sunflower seed flour	13.7 g	9 g	4.7 g	25.1 g	6.3 g	1 171
Dough 2	Entire batch; made with 1 cup sunflower seed flour + 1 cup nut flour	51.7 g	35.2 g	16.5 g	90.7 g	21.6 g	4 044
Dough 2	Entire batch; made with 1 cup sunflower seed flour + 1 cup flax meal	75.3 g	62.5 g	12.8 g	111.9 g	36.4 g	5 752

¾ cup water

60 g butter

2 cups sunflower seed flour (alternatively, you can use 1 cup sunflower seed flour and 1 cup golden or brown flax meal if making nachos or tacos)

1 tsp salt

1 Tbsp psyllium husk powder

1 egg

2 tsp baking powder

¼ cup sunflower seed flour or nut flour for sprinkling and handling the dough

In a medium-sized, heavy-bottomed saucepan, warm the water and butter together on medium heat. You don't want the water to boil before the butter has melted properly, so take things nice and slow.

Mix the 2 cups flour, salt and psyllium husk powder together in a separate bowl, making sure the psyllium is mixed in evenly.

As soon as the butter has melted and the water starts to boil, add the dry ingredients to the saucepan and stir until the mixture forms a ball of dough. Turn the heat to the lowest setting and cook the dough ball while moving it around in the saucepan for about 1 minute. You want the dough to have an elastic but firm-to-the-touch consistency.

Remove the saucepan from the heat and place the dough ball in a mixing bowl. Allow to cool for 5 minutes.

Now, break the egg into the mixing bowl with the dough ball and add the baking powder. Mix with an electric beater for about 1 minute. Scrape all the dough from the sides and beat and work into a soft dough ball. Sprinkle with a little of the extra flour and use your hands to shape the dough into a non-sticky, slightly glossy ball for 10–20 seconds. This is literally just to shape the dough; don't try to knead it like you would with glutinous doughs.

Wrap the dough ball in plastic wrap and pop into the freezer for 5 minutes or into the refrigerator for up to three days. Then simply shape it and bake it according to your chosen recipe.

DOUGH 3 (SWEET DOUGH)

USE THIS DOUGH FOR: SOFT PRETZELS (SWEET AND SAVOURY), CINNABON ROLLS, AFRICAN COFFEE CAKE (MONKEY BREAD), PIZZA PULL-APART BREAD, FOCACCIA, ROOSTERKOEK, CIABATTA, SANDWICH BREAD, BULL IN A BLANKET, KOEKSISTERS, POPTARTS, BRAAI PIE, VETKOEK AND SWEET BREAD.

RECIPE	PORTIONS	TOTAL CARBS	FIBRE	NET CARBS	FAT	PROTEIN	KJ
Dough 3	Entire batch; made with 2 cups sunflower seed flour	55.4 g	36 g	19.4 g	104.8 g	30.7 g	4 752
Dough 3	4; made with 2 cups sunflower seed flour	14.2 g	9 g	5.2 g	26.2 g	7.7 g	1 100
Dough 3	Entire batch; made with 1 cup sunflower seed flour + 1 cup nut flour	52.2 g	35.1 g	17.1 g	95.1 g	27.1 g	4 316
Dough 3	Entire batch; made with 2 cups nut flour	49 g	34.1 g	14.9 g	85.4 g	23.6 g	3 880

¾ cup water
60 g butter
2 cups sunflower seed flour (or use 1 cup sunflower seed flour and 1 cup nut flour of choice, see individual recipe suggestions)
¾ tsp salt
1 Tbsp xylitol
1 Tbsp psyllium husk powder
2 eggs
¼ cup sunflower seed flour or nut flour for sprinkling and handling the dough

In a medium-sized, heavy-bottomed saucepan, warm the water and butter together on medium heat. You don't want the water to boil before the butter has melted properly, so take things nice and slow.

Mix the 2 cups flour, salt, xylitol and psyllium husk powder together in a separate bowl, making sure the psyllium is mixed in evenly.

As soon as the butter has melted and the water starts to boil, add the dry ingredients to the saucepan and stir until the mixture forms a ball of dough. Turn the heat to the lowest setting and cook the dough ball while moving it around in the saucepan for about 1 minute. You want the dough to have an elastic but firm-to-the-touch consistency.

Remove the saucepan from the heat and place the dough ball in a mixing bowl. Allow to cool for 5 minutes.

Break the eggs into the mixing bowl with the dough ball and mix with an electric beater for about 1 minute. Scrape the dough from the sides and beat and work into a soft dough ball. Sprinkle with a little of the extra flour and use your hands to shape the dough into a non-sticky, slightly glossy ball for 10–20 seconds. This is literally just to shape the dough; don't try to knead it like glutinous doughs.

Wrap the dough ball in plastic wrap and pop into the freezer for 5 minutes or into the refrigerator for up to three days. Then simply shape it and bake it according to your chosen recipe.

DOUGH 4

THIS BUDGET-FRIENDLY ALTERNATIVE FOR DOUGHS 1 AND 3 IS A COCONUT FLOUR-BASED DOUGH FOR THOSE WHO USE IT AS THEIR FLOUR OF CHOICE.
USE THIS DOUGH FOR: PIZZA, PRETZELS, STUFFED BUNS, SWEET PIES, SAVOURY PIES AND MINI HAMBURGER BUNS.

RECIPE	PORTIONS	TOTAL CARBS	FIBRE	NET CARBS	FAT	PROTEIN	KJ
Dough 4	Entire batch	109.1 g	88.1 g	21 g	224.9 g	66.5 g	10 204

1 cup water
¾ cup butter
¾ cup coconut flour
¾ cup golden or brown flax meal
2 Tbsp ground chia seeds (made in a coffee grinder)
1 tsp salt
2 eggs
1 tsp baking powder
¼ cup flax meal or coconut flour for sprinkling and handling the dough (optional, as this dough is not as sticky as the others)

In a medium-sized, heavy-bottomed saucepan, warm the water and butter together on medium heat. You don't want the water to boil before the butter has melted properly, so take things nice and slow.

Mix the coconut flour, flax meal, chia seeds and salt together in a separate bowl, making sure the chia is mixed in evenly.

As soon as the butter has melted and the water starts to boil, add the dry ingredients to the saucepan and stir until the mixture forms a ball of dough. Turn the heat to the lowest setting and cook the dough ball while moving it around in the saucepan for about 1 minute. You want the dough to have an elastic but firm-to-the-touch consistency.

Remove the saucepan from the heat and place the dough ball in a mixing bowl. Allow to cool for 5 minutes.

Now, break the eggs into the mixing bowl with the dough ball, add the baking powder and mix with an electric beater for about 1 minute. Scrape all the dough from the sides and beat and work into a soft dough ball. Sprinkle with a little of the extra flour and use your hands to shape the dough into a non-sticky, slightly glossy ball for 10–20 seconds. This is literally just to shape the dough; don't try to knead it like you would with glutinous doughs.

Wrap the dough ball in plastic wrap and pop into the freezer for 5 minutes or into the refrigerator for up to three days. Then simply shape it and bake it according to your chosen recipe.

LEKKER TIPS
- Due to the very fibrous coconut flour, this dough does not handle with the same elasticity as doughs 1 and 3, but once you get the hang of it, it works like a charm and is still delicious.
- Doughs 1, 2, 3, 4 and 6 can be made ahead, wrapped in plastic wrap and refrigerated. They keep well in the refrigerator for 2–3 days. Alternatively, freeze some balls of dough wrapped in plastic wrap and thaw at room temperature when needed. You can also bake the desired recipe and freeze the end product for up to four weeks.

DOUGH 5

THIS BATTER IS A WINNER WHEN IT COMES TO A TRUSTY, QUICK, HIGH-FIBRE AND HEALTHY FAT, PROTEIN-RICH BREAD.
USE THIS DOUGH FOR: BRAAI SCONES, FRUIT MUFFINS, SAVOURY MUFFINS, BREADS AND HERBED BREAD.

RECIPE	PORTIONS	TOTAL CARBS	FIBRE	NET CARBS	FAT	PROTEIN	KJ
Dough 5	Entire batch	78 g	52 g	26 g	183 g	76 g	8 752

½ cup coconut flour
¼ cup golden flax meal
½ cup nut flour of choice
2 Tbsp ground chia seeds (made in a coffee grinder)
½ tsp bicarbonate of soda
½ tsp baking powder
1 tsp salt
½ cup melted salted butter
1 tsp vanilla extract
6 eggs
1 Tbsp apple cider vinegar
½ cup milk (or coconut milk, amasi, sour cream or fresh cream)

Place all the dry ingredients in a medium mixing bowl.

In a second mixing bowl, add all the liquid ingredients and give them a quick whisk.

Add the wet ingredients to the dry ingredients and stir for about 30 seconds, allowing the batter to firm up a bit.

Pour the batter into a baking paper-lined loaf pan or a 12-hole regular muffin pan, depending on your chosen recipe.

LEKKER TIPS

* For a white bread, use macadamia or almond flour as the nut flour. For a 'wholewheat' feel or 'bran'-type muffins, use pecan flour as the nut flour.
* Bread, scones and muffins can be frozen for up to six weeks.

Farm-style bread

THIS BREAD MAKES THE *BEST* TOASTED CHEESE-IN-A-PAN SANDWICHES. IT IS THE CLOSEST TO WHITE BREAD THAT I HAVE TASTED OR MANAGED TO MAKE SO FAR. IT IS SUPER HIGH IN FIBRE, BUT DOES NOT HAVE THE CONSISTENCY OF A WHOLEWHEAT- OR SEED-TYPE BREAD. WE DON'T EAT LOW-CARB BREAD EVERY DAY, WHICH MAKES A FARM-STYLE BREAD LIKE THIS A VERY SPECIAL MEAL INDEED.

RECIPE	PORTIONS	TOTAL CARBS	FIBRE	NET CARBS	FAT	PROTEIN	KJ
Farm-style bread	Entire batch	119.6 g	75 g	44.6 g	311.6 g	122.4 g	14 620

2 quantities Dough 5, with an extra 1 tsp salt (opposite)

Preheat the oven to 180 °C using the fan-assist function if your oven has one. Line a loaf pan with baking paper.

Prepare the batter as described in the recipe, but double up the quantities.

Place in the prepared loaf pan and bake for 1 hour (or slightly longer if you don't have a fan-assist function). Switch off the oven, then allow the bread to cool in the oven for 30 minutes before tipping it out onto a wire rack.

Allow the bread to cool completely before slicing thinly.

Yields 1 really large loaf of 7 x 2-slice servings

LEKKER TIPS
- Butter some slices on the outside and fill with your choice of grated mozzarella, onion, garlic, tomato, pesto or fresh herbs. In a pan on medium heat, toast both sides until nicely browned and the cheese has melted.
- *Braaibroodjies* and French toast are other wow options to try with this bread.

Braai scones

RECIPE	PORTIONS	TOTAL CARBS	FIBRE	NET CARBS	FAT	PROTEIN	KJ
Braai scones	1 scone	6.7 g	4.3 g	2.4 g	16.2 g	9.3 g	812

1 quantity Dough 5 (p. 20) – use macadamia or almond flour as the nut flour, or sunflower seed flour for a nut-free version
½ cup biltong powder (very dried biltong milled in a coffee grinder; this way you skip the preservatives)
1 heaped Tbsp chopped fresh chives
2 Tbsp finely grated Parmesan cheese

Preheat the oven to 180 °C. Butter a 12-square brownie pan or a 12-hole regular muffin pan.

Prepare the batter as described in the recipe, adding the biltong powder, chives and Parmesan when you mix the dry ingredients together. Scoop the batter into the prepared pan and bake in the oven for 20–25 minutes.

Yields 12 braai scones

Fruit muffins

RECIPE	PORTIONS	TOTAL CARBS	FIBRE	NET CARBS	FAT	PROTEIN	KJ
Berry	1 muffin	7.4 g	4.7 g	2.7 g	15.3 g	6.4 g	744
Apple cinnamon	1 muffin	7.6 g	4.5 g	3.1 g	15.3 g	6.4 g	744
Orange and choc	1 muffin	10 g	4.8 g	5.2 g	16.2 g	7.1 g	962
Carrot and nut	1 muffin	8.8 g	5.1 g	3.7 g	18.2 g	7.4 g	876
Pumpkin cinnamon	1 muffin	7.8 g	4.7 g	3.1 g	15.3 g	6.5 g	746

1 quantity Dough 5 (p. 20)*
2 Tbsp xylitol
Add any ONE of the following:
½ cup low-carb frozen berries (raspberries, strawberries, blackberries or blueberries)
½ cup grated apple plus 1 tsp ground cinnamon
Zest of 1 orange plus 4 blocks 85% dark chocolate, chopped
½ cup chopped nuts, ½ cup grated carrots and 1 tsp ground cinnamon
½ cup pumpkin purée, 1 tsp mixed spice and ½ tsp ground cinnamon

Preheat the oven to 180 °C. Butter a 12-hole regular muffin pan.

Prepare the batter as described in the recipe, adding the fruit option of choice when you add the wet ingredients to the dry ingredients. Scoop the batter into the prepared pan and bake for 20–25 minutes.

Yields 12 muffins

* I suggest pecan flour as the nut flour option.

Garlic, cheese and herb bread/muffins

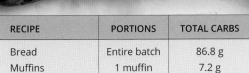

RECIPE	PORTIONS	TOTAL CARBS
Bread	Entire batch	86.8 g
Muffins	1 muffin	7.2 g

FIBRE	NET CARBS	FAT	PROTEIN	KJ
52.6 g	34.2 g	244 g	108 g	11 584
4.4 g	2.8 g	20 g	9 g	964

1 quantity Dough 5 (p. 20) – use macadamia,
almond or even sunflower seed flour as the nut
flour option
½ cup sour cream (or coconut cream for
a dairy-free option)
1 cup grated Cheddar cheese
1½ tsp crushed garlic
1 heaped Tbsp chopped fresh mixed herbs or 1 tsp
dried mixed herbs
Extra grated cheese and herbs for topping
(optional)

Preheat the oven to 180 °C. Butter a 12-square
brownie pan or 12-hole regular muffin pan, or line
a loaf pan with baking paper.

Prepare the batter as described in the recipe,
adding the sour cream, cheese, garlic and herbs to
the liquid mixture. Mix the wet ingredients into the
dry ingredients.

Scoop the batter into the prepared pan of
choice and bake. The muffins will take 20–25 minutes and the loaf will need 45 minutes. If using, top
the bread/muffins with extra cheese and herbs
5 minutes before you take them out of the oven.

Yields 12 muffins or 1 loaf

DOUGH 6
PIE CRUSTS, CRACKERS AND COOKIES

Sweet pie crust

USE FOR: FRIDGE TARTS, BAKED SWEET PIES, BARS AND CHEESECAKE CRUSTS

RECIPE	PORTIONS	TOTAL CARBS	FIBRE	NET CARBS	FAT	PROTEIN	KJ
Sweet pie crust	Entire batch	57.2 g	20.3 g	36.9 g	173 g	35 g	7 248

1 cup nut flour of choice or sunflower seed flour
1 cup desiccated coconut meal (regular desiccated coconut milled in a coffee grinder)
¼ tsp salt
1 tsp baking powder
105 g butter
2 Tbsp water
1 Tbsp gelatine powder
2 Tbsp xylitol
1 egg, beaten
1 tsp vanilla extract

Preheat the oven to 180 °C.

Place the flour, coconut meal, salt and baking powder in a small mixing bowl.

In a small saucepan on medium heat, warm the butter until completely melted. In a small bowl, add the water to the gelatine and allow to bloom for a few minutes.

Remove the butter from the heat and add the gelatine and xylitol. Stir with a whisk until well combined and completely dissolved. Add the gelatine mixture to the dry ingredients and start to mix. Add the beaten egg and vanilla to the mix. Mix by hand until the dough comes together a bit.

This batter has a very crumbly consistency, much like cookie-based crusts. Be sure to press it very firmly into the chosen mould in order to get an even base that will hold together perfectly. Bake for 15 minutes.

Yields:
1 springform round cheesecake crust (cover base with baking paper)
OR 2 x fridge tart shells made in round foil pans
OR 6 large cupcake shells made in silicone cupcake moulds
OR 24 mini shells made in mini cupcake silicone moulds
OR 1 cookie sheet pan (23 cm x 33 cm) crust base for bars or custard slices (line with baking paper)

LEKKER TIP
Add 2 Tbsp cocoa powder and an extra 1 tsp vanilla extract for a chocolate version.

Savoury pie crust

USE FOR: SUMMER TARTS, QUICHE, AND DEEP-DISH PIES FOR CRUST (USE DOUGH 1 FOR TOPPING)

RECIPE	PORTIONS	TOTAL CARBS	FIBRE	NET CARBS	FAT	PROTEIN	KJ
Savoury pie crust	Entire batch	34.8 g	20.3 g	14.5 g	180 g	45 g	7 392

1 cup nut flour of choice or sunflower seed flour
1 cup desiccated coconut meal (regular desiccated coconut milled in a coffee grinder)
2 Tbsp grated Parmesan cheese
¼ tsp garlic powder
¼ tsp salt
1 tsp baking powder
105 g butter
2 Tbsp water
1 Tbsp gelatine powder
1 egg, beaten

Preheat the oven to 180 °C.

Place the flour, coconut meal, Parmesan, garlic powder, salt and baking powder in a small mixing bowl.

In a small saucepan on medium heat, warm the butter until completely melted. In a small bowl, add the water to the gelatine and allow to bloom for a few minutes.

Remove the butter from the heat and add the gelatine. Stir with a whisk until well combined and completely dissolved. Add the gelatine mixture to the dry ingredients and start to mix. Add the beaten egg to the mix. Mix by hand until the dough comes together a bit.

This batter has a very crumbly consistency, much like cookie-based crusts. Be sure to press it very firmly into the chosen mould in order to get an even base that will hold together perfectly. Bake for 15 minutes.

Yields:
1 springform round cheesecake crust (cover base with baking paper)
OR 2 x fridge tart shells made in round foil pans
OR 6 large cupcake shells made in silicone cupcake moulds
OR 24 mini shells made in mini cupcake silicone moulds
OR 1 cookie sheet pan (23 cm x 33 cm) crust base for bars or savoury slices (line with baking paper)

Crackers

THESE CRACKERS ARE REALLY, *REALLY* CRISPY AND DELICIOUS.
THE ADDITION OF GELATINE GIVES THEM A SUPER FOOD BOOST.

RECIPE	PORTIONS	TOTAL CARBS	FIBRE	NET CARBS	FAT	PROTEIN	KJ
Crackers	1 round cracker	1.3 g	0.8 g	0.5 g	2 g	1.4 g	188

2 cups sunflower seed flour
(or 1 cup sunflower seed flour and
1 cup nut flour of choice)
1 tsp salt
2 Tbsp chopped fresh mixed herbs
of choice
1 tsp black pepper, lemon pepper,
chilli flakes, paprika, garlic flakes
or any spice of choice
½ tsp bicarbonate of soda
125 g butter
¼ cup milk
2 Tbsp water
1 Tbsp gelatine powder
1 egg, beaten
1 cup grated Cheddar cheese or
2–3 Tbsp grated Parmesan cheese
2–3 Tbsp sesame seeds for
rolling or sprinkling onto cookies
(optional)

Preheat the oven to 180 °C. Line a baking sheet with baking paper.

Place the flour, salt, herbs, spice and bicarbonate of soda in a mixing bowl. In a small saucepan on medium heat, warm the butter and milk together until the butter has melted. Don't let the milk boil.

In a small bowl, add the water to the gelatine and allow to bloom for a few minutes.

Remove the milk mixture from the heat and add the gelatine. Stir with a whisk until well combined and completely dissolved. Add the gelatine milk mix to the dry ingredients and start to mix. Add the beaten egg and cheese. Mix by hand until the dough comes together to form a ball.

Place a sheet of plastic wrap on a cutting board and shape the dough into a sausage about 30 cm long, using the sides of the plastic wrap to help shape the buttery, sticky dough. Wrap and allow the dough so set and chill in the freezer for a few minutes.

Dip the dough in sesame seeds, wrap again in plastic wrap and chill in the freezer for 5–8 minutes, then cut into 5–7 mm-thick slices. Alternatively, roll the dough sausage onto a baking paper-lined 23 cm x 33 cm pan using your rolling pin, and pre-cut into squares.

Bake for about 25 minutes until the cheese seeps through to the top of the crackers and appears melted, bubbly and brown. The crackers should also have toasty browned edges. These crackers will harden upon cooling.

Gently break into pre-cut squares while still warm to the touch.

Yields 48 round crackers or 88 bite-size square crackers

LEKKER TIPS

- The flavour profile combinations with these crackers are endless! Personally I like the following combinations (add when method calls for herbs and spices):
  1 Tbsp chopped fresh rosemary + 1 Tbsp freshly ground black pepper.
  1 Tbsp chopped fresh thyme + 1 Tbsp chopped fresh chives.
  1 tsp chilli flakes + 1 tsp crushed garlic.

Cookies

AFTER MANY SLEEPLESS NIGHTS OF PONDERINGS AND PROBABLY 25 KG OF VARIOUS FLOURS, IT IS WITH ALMOST MATERNAL PRIDE THAT I PRESENT YOU WITH THE *HARD, DUNKABLE* COOKIE BASE THAT MAKES A SNAP WHEN YOU BREAK IT IN HALF! GET READY TO WELCOME ALL SORTS OF GRANDMA AND HOLIDAY COOKIE MEMORIES BACK INTO YOUR KITCHEN.

RECIPE	PORTIONS	TOTAL CARBS	FIBRE	NET CARBS	FAT	PROTEIN	KJ
Cookies	Entire batch	22.4 g	8 g	14.4 g	154 g	41 g	6 360

2 cups sunflower seed flour
(or 1 cup sunflower seed flour and
1 cup nut flour of choice)
½ tsp salt
½ tsp bicarbonate of soda
125 g butter
¼ cup milk
2 Tbsp water
1 Tbsp gelatine powder
6 Tbsp xylitol
1 egg, beaten
1 tsp vanilla extract

Preheat the oven to 180 °C. Line a baking sheet with baking paper. Place the flour, salt and bicarbonate of soda in a mixing bowl.

In a small saucepan on medium heat, warm the butter and milk together until the butter has melted. Don't let the milk boil.

In a small bowl, add the water to the gelatine and allow to bloom for a few minutes. Remove the milk mixture from the heat and add the gelatine and xylitol. Stir with a whisk until well combined and completely dissolved.

Add the gelatine milk mixture to the dry ingredients and start to mix. Add the beaten egg and vanilla to the mix. Mix by hand until the dough comes together to form a ball.

Place a sheet of plastic wrap on a cutting board and shape the dough into a sausage, using the sides of the plastic wrap to help shape the buttery, sticky dough. Wrap and allow the dough to set and chill in the freezer for a few minutes.

Now you can either slice the dough into thin rounds and sprinkle them with a bit of xylitol (optional) or simply roll the dough into 2–3 cm balls and dip them in a bit of xylitol (optional). Space apart on the prepared baking sheet, flatten the balls with a fork and bake for 20–25 minutes or until the cookies turn toasty. These cookies harden upon cooling.

Alternatively, place a sheet of plastic wrap on a cutting board, top with the dough and a second sheet of plastic wrap, and roll out the dough until 5 mm thick. Cut out cookies using cookie cutters. Bake for 15–20 minutes.

Yield depends on the format and size of your cookies.

DOUGH 7

USE THIS DOUGH FOR: WAFFLES AND DOUGHNUTS.

WAFFLES AND MINI DOUGHNUTS

THESE ARE PERFECT FOR THOSE WAFFLE AND DOUGHNUT MACHINES THAT YOU PACKED AWAY SINCE LIVING A LOW-CARB LIFESTYLE. BLOW OFF THE DUST AND PREPARE TO BE AMAZED AT THE UNLIMITED NEW POSSIBILITIES THIS DOUGH AND ALL ITS VARIATIONS WILL BRING.

Sweet dough base

RECIPE	PORTIONS	TOTAL CARBS	FIBRE	NET CARBS	FAT	PROTEIN	KJ
Sweet vanilla	1 waffle	5.6 g	1.7 g	3.9 g	10.1 g	5.8 g	540
Chocolate	1 waffle	7 g	2.5 g	4.5 g	10.5 g	6.3 g	564
Pumpkin	1 waffle	8 g	2.6 g	5.4 g	10.2 g	6.1 g	580

4 eggs
½ block or 125 g cream cheese
1¼ cups macadamia, almond or sunflower seed flour
¼ cup coconut flour
¼ cup xylitol
¼ tsp salt
2 tsp baking powder
1 tsp vanilla extract
Up to ½ cup full-cream milk or coconut milk
Coconut oil, for coating waffle pan

Place the eggs and cream cheese in a blender and blend together.

Mix all the dry ingredients together. Mix the egg and cream cheese mixture into the dry ingredients and stir well. (Some coconut flours are a bit more dense than others so you may need to add some milk to get the batter to the correct scoopable consistency.)

Follow waffle pan or doughnut machine instructions. I leave my batter in for about 30 seconds longer, once the light turns on to signal it is ready to take out. This yields a crispier waffle crust. I also use a little less batter and only scoop a few spoonfuls in the centre of my square waffle pan. This way I end up with round, thick Belgian-like waffles that work great as a hamburger base.

Yields 6–8 waffles (depending on your waffle iron) or 36–48 mini doughnuts

LEKKER TIPS

- This recipe makes lovely plain sweet waffles. Serve with caramel sauce (p. 165) and whipped cream or add blueberries or dark choc chips to the waffle batter to make them a bit more exciting.
- For a **Chocolate dough base**, add ¼ cup cocoa powder to the dry ingredients. Serve with caramel sauce and cream or orange zest-infused cream.
- For a **Pumpkin spice dough base**, add 1 cup cooked, mashed and drained pumpkin, 1 tsp ground cinnamon and ¾ tsp mixed spice to the batter. These are amazing served with a dash of cinnamon mixed with xylitol, some butter, crème fraîche and streaky bacon.

Savoury dough base

RECIPE	PORTIONS	TOTAL CARBS	FIBRE	NET CARBS	FAT	PROTEIN	KJ
Savoury	1 waffle	6.1 g	3.7 g	2.4 g	13.2 g	7.3 g	544
Variation 1	1 waffle	6.6 g	3.9 g	2.7 g	16.1 g	11.7 g	836
Variation 2	1 waffle	6.6 g	3.9 g	2.7 g	14 g	8 g	700
Variation 3	1 waffle	7.3 g	4.1 g	3.2 g	15 g	9 g	772
Variation 4	1 waffle	7.2 g	4.1 g	3.1 g	18 g	11 g	900

4 eggs

½ block or 125 g cream cheese

1 cup sunflower seed flour or nut flour

¼ cup coconut flour (preferably store bought)

¼ cup golden flax meal (or brown, but golden yields a light colour to the dough and a much milder taste)

½ tsp salt

2 tsp baking powder

Up to ½ cup full-cream milk or coconut milk

Coconut oil, for coating waffle pan

Now add ONE of the following savoury flavour options:

SAVOURY OPTION 1

1 cup dry biltong powder (made in a coffee grinder)

2 Tbsp grated Parmesan cheese

1 Tbsp chopped fresh thyme

A good grind black pepper

SAVOURY OPTION 2

1 cup finely chopped fresh spinach

1 tsp crushed garlic

¼ cup crumbled feta cheese

Black pepper to taste

SAVOURY OPTION 3

1–2 spring onions, finely chopped

2 Tbsp chopped sun-dried tomato

¼ cup crumbled blue cheese

1 Tbsp chopped fresh mixed herbs

A good grind black pepper

SAVOURY OPTION 4

1 cup grated Cheddar cheese

1 Tbsp chopped fresh chives

½ tsp chilli flakes (optional)

A good grind black pepper

Place the eggs and cream cheese in a blender and blend together.

Mix all the dry ingredients together. Mix the egg and cream cheese mixture into the dry ingredients and stir well.

Follow waffle pan or doughnut machine instructions. I leave my batter in for about 30 seconds longer once the light turns on to signal it is ready to take out. This yields a crispier waffle crust. I also use a little less batter and only scoop a few spoonfuls in the centre of my square waffle pan. This way I end up with round, thick Belgian-like waffles that work great as a hamburger base.

Yields 6–8 waffles (depending on your waffle iron) or 36–48 mini doughnuts

DOUGH 8

(KIDDIE OR ANTI-ALLERGEN DOUGH)

I NAMED THIS ONE THE SWEETHEART DOUGH BECAUSE IT IS NUT FREE, EGG FREE AND CAN BE DAIRY FREE IF YOU SWAP THE BUTTER FOR COCONUT OIL. BUT BE WARNED: IT TASTES LIKE FRESHLY BAKED HOT CROSS BUNS WHEN JUST TAKEN OUT OF THE OVEN. THIS IS ABSOLUTELY ONE OF MY FAVOURITES AND MY TWIN GIRLS AGREE! I PRACTICALLY RAISED THEM ON THESE FROM ABOUT EIGHT MONTHS OF AGE.
USE THIS DOUGH FOR: SWEETHEART SANDWICHES, SWEETHEART SOFT BABY BAGELS, SWEETHEART CINNAMON ROLLS, SWEETHEART BUGS AND BUTTERFLIES, AND SWEETHEART CUSTARD SLICES (EGG YOLK ONLY).

RECIPE	PORTIONS	TOTAL CARBS	FIBRE	NET CARBS	FAT	PROTEIN	KJ
Dough 8	Entire batch	66 g	39 g	27 g	96 g	20 g	4 468

¾ cup water
60 g butter or coconut oil
2 cups sunflower seed flour
½ tsp salt
1 Tbsp xylitol
1 Tbsp psyllium husk powder
50 g cooked pumpkin cubes, puréed
50 g cooked, peeled apple cubes, puréed
1 tsp vanilla extract
¼ cup sunflower seed flour for sprinkling and handling the dough

In a medium-sized, heavy-bottomed saucepan, warm the water and butter together on medium heat. You don't want the water to boil before the butter has melted properly, so take things nice and slow.

Mix the 2 cups flour, salt, xylitol and psyllium husk powder together in a separate bowl, making sure the psyllium is mixed in evenly.

As soon as the butter has melted and the water starts to boil, add the dry ingredients to the saucepan and stir until the mixture forms a ball of dough. Turn the heat to the lowest setting and cook the dough ball while moving it around in the saucepan for about 1 minute. You want the dough to have an elastic but firm-to-the-touch consistency.

Remove the saucepan from the heat and place the dough ball in a mixing bowl. Allow to cool for 5 minutes.

Now, add the purées and the vanilla into the mixing bowl with the dough ball and mix with an electric beater for about 1 minute. Scrape all the dough from the sides and beat and work into a soft dough ball. Sprinkle with a little of the extra flour and use your hands to shape the dough into a non-sticky, slightly glossy ball for 10–20 seconds. This is literally just to shape the dough; don't try to knead it like you would with glutinous doughs.

Wrap the dough ball in plastic wrap and pop into the freezer for 5 minutes or into the refrigerator for up to three days. Then simply shape it and bake it according to your chosen recipe.

Around the world
in 18 meals

Snoek braai and pumpkin fritter pie
(South Africa)

SNOEK IS CONSIDERED TO BE A TRULY SOUTH AFRICAN DISH. THIS FISH HAS A SAVOURY, SMOKY TASTE AND IS USUALLY MARINATED WITH LOADS OF APRICOT JAM, BUTTER AND GARLIC. THE WEST COAST LOCALS WILL ALSO TELL YOU THAT NO SNOEK BRAAI IS COMPLETE WITHOUT SWEET POTATOES AND HOME-MADE BREAD WITH ... MORE JAM! THIS IS MY VERSION OF THE SAME ELEMENTS AND TASTE PROFILES MINUS THE EXCESSIVE CARBS.

RECIPE	PORTIONS	TOTAL CARBS	FIBRE	NET CARBS	FAT	PROTEIN	KJ
Snoek braai	1	11.1 g	2.9 g	8 g	34 g	40 g	2 104

PUMPKIN FRITTER PIE
Butter for greasing
1 x 250 g tub cream cheese, at room temperature
6 eggs
1 tsp vanilla extract
½ cup fresh cream
1 x 500 g packet cubed pumpkin, cooked and drained
2 tsp baking powder
¼ tsp salt
Xylitol and ground cinnamon for sprinkling

SNOEK MARINADE
100 g butter, melted
½ medium red onion, diced
1 Tbsp xylitol
1 tsp garlic, crushed
3 Tbsp lemon juice
Salt and pepper to taste

1 whole snoek, butterflied

Make the pumpkin fritter pie first. Preheat the oven to 180 °C. Grease a medium-sized ovenproof dish with butter.

In a food processor or blender, mix all the ingredients, except the xylitol and cinnamon, to a very runny consistency. Pour the mixture into the prepared dish.

Bake for 30–40 minutes or until brown and some cracks appear in the surface. Allow to cool and then sprinkle with xylitol and cinnamon just before serving.

To make the marinade, melt the butter in a small saucepan on medium heat, and then pour all but about 1 Tbsp worth into a blender. Sauté the onion in the leftover butter. Add the xylitol and allow the onion to caramelise a bit.

Place the onion and the remaining marinade ingredients into the blender and blend until smooth and thick.

Place the open snoek onto a double-sided grid and, before closing the grid around the fish, paint a generous layer of marinade over the inside of the fish. Place the grid onto medium-hot coals with the fish skin side down. Continue basting with the marinade on both sides. Cook for 15 minutes or until the fish is flaky. Serve with the pumpkin fritter pie.

Yields 6–8 portions

LEKKER TIP
I would serve this dish with a lovely fibre-filled salad, but if you really want to be authentic, serve it with Braai Scones (p. 22) or Sweet Bread (p. 18).

Braai pie (South Africa)

MY FAMILY WOULD EAT THIS EVERY DAY IF THEY COULD (NOT THAT THEY SHOULD...). IT SHOULD ALSO BE KNOWN AS 'BRIBE' PIE, AS THIS IS THE CARD YOU CAN PLAY WHEN YOU WANT CHORES DONE AND ROOMS CLEANED IN RECORD TIME ... SERIOUSLY THOUGH, I HAVE MADE THIS FOR GUESTS MANY TIMES BEFORE AND IT GOES SO WELL WITH A BRAAI EVEN THOUGH YOU MAKE IT IN THE OVEN. THIS IS *BRAAIBROODJIE* (TOASTIE) MEETS GARLIC BREAD IN A LOW-CARB MARRIAGE MADE IN HEAVEN. SERVE WITH LAMB RIBS HOT OFF THE BRAAI AND YOUR FAVOURITE HIGH-FIBRE SALAD.

RECIPE	PORTIONS	TOTAL CARBS	FIBRE	NET CARBS	FAT	PROTEIN	KJ
Braai pie	1	9.8 g	6 g	3.8 g	30.7 g	15.5 g	1 444

1 quantity Dough 3, using 2 cups sunflower seed flour for best results (p. 18)
1 Tbsp crushed garlic (or more to taste)
2–3 cups grated cheese of choice (more is better)
1 egg, beaten
Salt to taste

Preheat the oven to 180 °C.

Prepare the dough as described in the recipe. Divide the chilled dough ball into two equal parts. Place one piece on a sheet of baking paper and the other on a chopping board covered with plastic wrap. Using a rolling pin, roll out both pieces into 3–4 mm-thick circles. Make the plastic wrap circle a tad smaller than the baking paper one.

Place the baking paper base onto a baking sheet. Spread garlic evenly over the base and then cover it with cheese.

Slip your hand under the plastic wrap base and, in one quick motion, tip the base on top of the cheese base. Carefully peel off the plastic wrap and then pinch and turn up the edges. Brush with the beaten egg wash and top with a few grinds of salt.

Bake for 20–25 minutes or until the top layer is golden brown and the base is crusty and no longer sticks to the baking paper.

Place the braai pie on a cutting board and cut into diagonal strips or pizza-like slices.

Yields 6 portions

Rooibos ginger-lime chicken (South Africa)

RECIPE	PORTIONS	TOTAL CARBS	FIBRE	NET CARBS	FAT	PROTEIN	KJ
Rooibos chicken	1	31.6 g	12.4 g	19.2 g	27.7 g	39.3 g	2 064

4 chicken thighs
4 chicken drumsticks
2 Tbsp coconut oil
Salt and black pepper to taste
8 rooibos tea bags steeped in
2 cups boiling water (or any citrus-
flavoured rooibos tea)
Zest and juice of 1 lime
½ x 400 ml can coconut cream
1 thumb-size piece fresh ginger,
grated
½ tsp crushed garlic
Handful chopped fresh coriander
leaves
2 medium sweet potatoes, cubed
(for a lower carb option use
400 g pumpkin)
2 medium brinjals, cubed
½ head cauliflower, roughly
chopped

Preheat the oven to 190 °C.

In a heavy-bottomed saucepan or Dutch oven, brown the chicken pieces in the coconut oil for 5–7 minutes. Add salt and pepper.

Remove the tea bags from the water, squeezing out all the liquid. Stir the lime juice and zest, coconut cream, ginger, garlic and coriander into the tea and pour into the saucepan. Arrange the veggies around the chicken pieces, put on the lid and bake for 20–25 minutes with the lid on.

Remove the lid and bake for another 15–20 minutes to reduce the liquid. Serve in deep bowls.

Yields 4–6 satisfying portions

LEKKER TIP
Use leftovers or double up this dish, debone the chicken and use as a pie filling along with Dough 3 (p. 18).

Smoky cabbage casserole (South Africa)

RECIPE	PORTIONS	TOTAL CARBS	FIBRE	NET CARBS	FAT	PROTEIN	KJ
Cabbage casserole	1	13.2 g	4 g	9.2 g	60 g	36 g	2 984

1 Tbsp fresh thyme leaves
¼ cup melted butter or coconut oil
1 head cabbage, sliced into rounds 1–2 cm thick
Salt and black pepper to taste
½ tsp crushed garlic
500 g boerewors (or sausage of choice)
1 x 200 g packet streaky bacon, diced
1 x 250 g tub crème fraîche
1 cup fresh cream or coconut cream
4 eggs
2 egg yolks
½ tsp grated nutmeg

Preheat the oven to 190 °C.

Stir the thyme leaves into the melted butter. Drizzle 2 Tbsp of the butter into a large ovenproof dish and arrange the cabbage slices on the melted butter. Give a good grind of salt and pepper and sprinkle over the garlic.

Cut the boerewors into smaller pieces and squeeze the filling out onto a chopping board. Cut or break the boerewors into 2 cm chunks and arrange these and the bacon pieces over the cabbage layer. Drizzle the rest of the butter over the cabbage and meat layer. Bake for 15 minutes.

Mix the crème fraîche, cream, eggs and egg yolks together and whisk well. Pour the custard mixture over the cabbage and meat. Return to the oven for 30 minutes until it starts to brown and set. Sprinkle with nutmeg before serving.

Yields 6 portions

Soft pretzel burgers and green bean fries (USA)

RECIPE	PORTIONS	TOTAL CARBS	FIBRE	NET CARBS	FAT	PROTEIN	KJ
Pretzel burgers	1 burger	21 g	11 g	10 g	50 g	60 g	1 750

SOFT PRETZELS

1 quantity Dough 3, made with
1 cup nut flour + 1 cup sunflower
seed flour (or just sunflower seed
flour) (p. 18)
1 egg, beaten
1 cup grated Cheddar or
mozzarella cheese
2 Tbsp chopped fresh mixed
herbs (your favourites or oregano,
thyme, chives and parsley)
Chilli flakes (optional)

BURGERS

700–800 g beef mince or 6 chicken
breast fillets
2 Tbsp BBQ spice (sugar-free)
4 Tbsp coconut oil for frying
12 sweet lettuce leaves
6 slices tomato
1 medium red onion, sautéed
Carb-smart 1000 island sauce
6 slices cheese
12 slices lowest carb count pickle

GREEN BEAN FRIES

700 g fresh green beans
2 Tbsp butter
Salt and pepper

First make the pretzels. Preheat the oven to 180 °C. Line two baking sheets with baking paper. Butter the baking paper lightly.

Prepare the dough as described in the recipe. Take the chilled dough ball and place onto a chopping board wrapped in a layer of plastic wrap. Using both hands, roll the dough ball into an 18 cm-long sausage. Cut into six equal pieces. Now roll each piece into a 44 cm-rope. Place a rope onto the greased baking sheet and twist into a pretzel shape. Repeat with each piece of dough.

Brush each pretzel with beaten egg and then generously cover with the cheese, herbs and chilli, if using. Bake for 12–15 minutes or until the pretzel is firm and the cheese is melted and brown.

For the burgers, divide the beef mince into six equal portions, roll into a tight ball and press between your hands to form an elongated patty that will fit onto the shape of the pretzels. Sprinkle BBQ spice on both sides of the patties. In a pan on medium to high heat, fry the patties in the coconut oil for 3–4 minutes a side, turning once or twice or according to preference.

For the green bean fries, sauté the green beans for 4–5 minutes in 2 Tbsp butter until soft with a slight crunch. Add salt and pepper to taste.

Assemble the pretzel burger starting with a pretzel wrong side up. Follow with a layer of lettuce, tomato and onion and a squeeze of 1000 island sauce. Add the patty next, top with cheese and finish with a pickle. Alternatively, slice each pretzel in half horizontally to create a top and bottom 'bun'. Serve the green bean fries on the side.

Yields 6 burgers

Flammkuchen (France and Germany)

THIS GERMAN/FRENCH VERSION OF PIZZA IS BEYOND AMAZING! IT IS A FAMILY FAVOURITE IN OUR HOUSE AND SO EASY TO MAKE.

RECIPE	PORTIONS	TOTAL CARBS
Flammkuchen	1	20 g

FIBRE	NET CARBS	FAT	PROTEIN	KJ
10 g	10 g	73 g	32 g	3 392

1 quantity Dough 2 (p. 17) – it works really well with
2 cups sunflower seed flour as a base or substitute
with 1 cup nut flour
250 g streaky bacon, roughly chopped
1 medium red onion, thinly sliced
1 Tbsp coconut oil or butter
1 x 250 g tub crème fraîche
½ cup thick sour cream
½ tsp ground nutmeg or grated whole nutmeg
1 Tbsp fresh thyme leaves
Salt and black pepper to taste

Preheat the oven to the highest temperature.
Prepare the dough as described in the recipe. Divide the chilled dough ball into two large or four smaller portions. Place each portion on its own sheet of baking paper and roll into a circle or rustic oval using a rolling pin. You need this dough base to be very thin, at least 4 mm or slightly thinner if you can. Bake the bases for 4–5 minutes on the baking paper.

In a frying pan on medium heat, sweat the bacon and onion in the coconut oil for 1–2 minutes.

Mix the crème fraîche and sour cream together and spread evenly onto the bases. Sprinkle nutmeg, thyme, salt and pepper on the crème fraîche topping. Arrange bacon pieces and onion on the bases and bake for another 5–8 minutes, or until crispy, directly on the baking paper on the wire oven racks.

Yields 4 portions

Baby marrow bolognaise (Italy)

SERVE WITH BRAAI PIE (P. 34) CUT INTO STRIPS LIKE GARLIC BREAD AND A LOVELY PLAIN GREEN SALAD.

RECIPE	PORTIONS	TOTAL CARBS	FIBRE	NET CARBS	FAT	PROTEIN	KJ
Bolognaise	1	10 g	3 g	7 g	24 g	58 g	1 940

BOLOGNAISE SAUCE

2 Tbsp coconut oil

1 medium red onion, finely diced

1 kg beef mince

2 Tbsp chopped fresh herbs of choice or parsley, oregano, chives and thyme

1 tsp crushed garlic (or more to taste)

1½ Tbsp BBQ spice (sugar-free)

1 x 400 ml can chopped tomatoes in juice

2 Tbsp xylitol

Salt and black pepper to taste

BABY MARROW SPAGHETTI

2 Tbsp butter or coconut oil for frying

1 kg baby marrows, made into spaghetti using a spiralizer

Salt to taste

Grated Parmesan or other hard cheese for garnishing

For the bolognaise sauce, heat the coconut oil in a heavy-bottomed saucepan and sauté the onion until soft. Add the mince, herbs, garlic and BBQ spice and brown. Add the tomatoes and xylitol and then taste to see if more salt or pepper is required. Simmer and reduce for 10–12 minutes, and then remove from heat.

As soon as the meat sauce is ready, prepare the baby marrow spaghetti. Heat the butter in a heavy-bottomed pan on medium-high heat. Add all the baby marrow spaghetti and lightly stir and sauté the veggie pasta for 2–3 minutes. You don't want them too soggy, so aim for soft with a slight crunch.

Pile the baby marrow spaghetti onto plates, top with meat sauce, garnish with cheese and enjoy!

Yields 4–6 portions

Tuscan fish dish (Italy)

RECIPE	PORTIONS	TOTAL CARBS	FIBRE	NET CARBS	FAT	PROTEIN	KJ
Tuscan fish dish	1	20 g	10 g	10 g	72 g	53 g	3 600

SAUCE

2 Tbsp chopped fresh herbs of choice or parsley, oregano, chives, thyme and rosemary

1 tsp crushed garlic (or more to taste)

16 black olives, pitted

2 Tbsp xylitol

2 x 400 ml cans chopped tomatoes in juice

Salt and black pepper to taste

FISH

4 Tbsp grated Parmesan cheese

8 Tbsp coconut flour

Salt and pepper to taste

½ tsp garlic powder

6 eggs

4 thick-cut hake fillets (about 175 g each)

½ cup coconut oil for frying

ASPARAGUS

2 Tbsp butter

24 asparagus spears

Salt and black pepper

Avocado oil, lemon zest and fresh basil leaves for garnishing

For the sauce, place all the ingredients in a heavy-bottomed sauce-pan on low to medium heat, and allow to infuse, simmer and reduce slowly to a thick sauce. Stir occasionally.

For the fish, mix the Parmesan, flour, seasoning and garlic powder in a deep dish plate. Whisk the eggs and pour into another deep dish plate.

Heat the coconut oil in a large heavy-bottomed pan on medium-high heat. Dip the hake fillets, one by one, into the egg, then roll in the flour mix and one more time in the egg. Add two hake fillets to the pan, skin side down, and fry for 3–5 minutes or until golden brown underneath. Turn over and fry for another 3–4 minutes. Repeat the process with the remaining two fillets.

Start the asparagus as soon as you start your second batch of hake fillets. Heat the butter in a separate heavy-bottomed pan on medium-high heat and sauté the asparagus for 3–4 minutes. Season to taste.

Dish up a serving of asparagus and top with a scoop of sauce. Position the hake on top of the sauce. Garnish with a drizzle of avo oil, lemon zest and fresh basil leaves.

Yields 4 filling portions

> **LEKKER TIP**
> When using coconut flour as a coating, it is better to dip into the egg first, then the flour and then the egg again.

Creamy spinach and brinjal lasagne
(Italy)

THIS PRETTY STRAIGHTFORWARD LASAGNE CONSISTS OF FOUR ELEMENTS: THE CREAMY SPINACH, THE SLIGHTLY SAUCY MEAT, THE EGG MIX AND CHEESE TOPPING, AND THE BRINJAL ROUNDS. YOU CAN SPICE UP THE MEAT HOWEVER YOU LIKE, AS LONG AS IT IS NOT TOO SAUCY.

RECIPE	PORTIONS	TOTAL CARBS	FIBRE	NET CARBS	FAT	PROTEIN	KJ
Lasagne	1	12.2 g	5.6 g	6.6 g	30.6 g	57 g	2 216

½ cup coconut oil, lard or rendered fat

2 large brinjals, cut into 1 cm rounds

1 kg mince of choice

1 Tbsp BBQ spice (sugar-free)

Salt and black pepper to taste

3 Tbsp chopped fresh mixed herbs

2 x 50 g sachets tomato paste

1 Tbsp xylitol

2 tsp crushed garlic

¼ cup water

2 x 300 g packets Swiss chard or spinach, centre stalks removed

1 cup fresh cream

½ block or 125 g cream cheese

3 eggs

1 cup milk

1 cup grated mozzarella cheese

1 cup grated Cheddar cheese

Preheat the oven to 190 °C. Place the coconut oil in a large baking tray and pop it into the oven until melted. Remove the tray from the oven and arrange all the brinjal rounds on the tray. Sprinkle lightly with salt. Pop into the oven for about 15 minutes until tender.

Meanwhile, brown the mince in a heavy-bottomed saucepan and then add the BBQ spice, salt and pepper, herbs, tomato paste, xylitol, garlic and water.

In a separate saucepan, boil/steam the spinach in a small amount of salted water. Just after the spinach reaches the wilted stage, drain the excess water, add the cream and cream cheese and allow the mixture to thicken and reduce for about 5 minutes while stirring gently.

Whisk the eggs and milk in a bowl.

In a large ovenproof dish, arrange half the brinjals in a single layer. Spread half of the mince on top of the brinjal layer, followed by all the creamy spinach. Then pack the rest of the brinjals on top of the spinach, followed by another layer of meat. Sprinkle the cheeses over the top and pour the egg mixture evenly over the entire dish. Bake for 25–35 minutes.

Serve with a beautiful green salad and be sure to save some for the next day's lunchbox. It is divine eaten cold, too.

Yields 4–6 portions

Swedish meatballs and gravy on cauli mash (Sweden)

AROMATIC SWEDISH MEATBALLS WITH AN UNCONVENTIONAL GRAVY THAT IS AS HEARTY BUT MUCH HEALTHIER THAN ANY OF ITS FLOUR- OR STARCH-FILLED COUSINS.

RECIPE	PORTIONS	TOTAL CARBS	FIBRE	NET CARBS	FAT	PROTEIN	KJ
Swedish meatballs	1	19.7 g	8 g	11.7 g	28 g	57 g	2 216

MEATBALLS

1 kg beef mince or beef and pork blend
Salt and pepper to taste
1 small onion, chopped
1 tsp ground nutmeg
1 tsp ground cardamom
1 egg yolk
3 Tbsp coconut oil for frying

GRAVY

6 medium baby marrows, grated
1 large brinjal, cubed
1 small red onion, chopped
3 Tbsp butter
¼ tsp crushed garlic (optional)
¼ tsp paprika
Salt and black pepper to taste
1½ cups beef broth or stock
¼ cup fresh cream or coconut cream

CAULI MASH

1 large head cauliflower, roughly chopped
1½ cups water
Salt and black pepper to taste
¼ cup fresh cream or coconut cream
A generous knob of butter

Handful chopped fresh parsley for garnishing

For the meatballs, mix together the mince, seasoning, onion, nutmeg, cardamom and egg yolk and roll into medium-sized balls. In a saucepan on medium to high heat, fry the meatballs in the coconut oil, turning often, until nicely browned all round. Remove from the pan and set aside.

Using the same pan for the gravy, sauté the baby marrows, brinjal and onion in the pan juices untill soft. Add the butter, garlic, paprika and seasoning as soon as the veggies start to brown. Add the cold broth to a blender. Add the cooked veggies to the blender and blend for 20 seconds. Return the puréed gravy to the pan, add the cream and allow to simmer and reduce slightly. Add the meatballs as soon as the gravy starts to thicken.

In a separate saucepan, cook the cauliflower in the water until soft. Add salt and pepper to taste. Drain the water, then add the cream and butter. Purée with a stick blender.

Serve the meatballs and gravy on a bed of cauli mash, garnished with parsley.

Yields 4–6 portions

Fish tacos and tangy cabbage slaw
(Mexico)

RECIPE	PORTIONS	TOTAL CARBS	FIBRE	NET CARBS	FAT	PROTEIN	KJ
Fish tacos	1 taco	24.3 g	14.8 g	9.5 g	27.6 g	8.4 g	1 536

TACO SHELLS

1 quantity Dough 2, made with
1 cup sunflower seed flour + 1 cup
golden or brown flax meal (p. 17)
1 tsp salt
¼ tsp paprika
¼ tsp chilli flakes (optional)
½ tsp onion flakes (optional)
¼ tsp dried mixed herbs

FILLING

⅓ cup avocado oil
2 tsp fish herbs and spices
1 Tbsp chopped fresh dill or 1 tsp
dried dill
½ tsp white pepper
½ tsp crushed garlic
Juice of ½ lemon
500 g hake fillets
1 avocado
½ cup sour cream
¼ tsp ground cumin

TANGY CABBAGE SLAW

¼ head cabbage, thinly sliced
½ small red cabbage, thinly sliced
1 medium red onion, thinly sliced
Juice of ½ lemon
Handful roughly chopped fresh
coriander leaves (optional)
2 Tbsp olive oil
Pinch chilli flakes
1 tsp xylitol
Salt and black pepper to taste
Grind of preferred mixed herb salt

Preheat the oven to 180 °C.

Prepare the dough as described in the recipe, adding the spices and dried herbs to the dry ingredients before adding it to the butter-water mixture.

Line a large chopping board or flat surface with plastic wrap and use a rolling pin to roll out the chilled dough into a rectangle 3–4 mm thick. Using a small side plate or saucer, cut out circles from the dough. Form another ball with the offcut pieces and repeat the process until you have used all of the dough. You need six circles for this recipe.

Use the bottom layer of plastic wrap as a support to lift and peel off the circles and place them onto a square double-folded piece of baking paper, just a bit bigger than the taco circle. Place each circle paper side down over two rungs of your wire oven rack and allow the sides to dangle down. You will immediately see this takes the shape of a taco shell.

Bake for 10–15 minutes or until crisp and slightly browned. Gently remove each shell from the rack and allow to cool standing upright.

While the tacos are in the oven, marinate the hake fillets. Mix the oil, herbs and spices, garlic and lemon juice in a bowl and drizzle over the fish fillets. Allow the fish to marinate in the refrigerator for 15 minutes.

Peel and cut the avo into thin slices and dish the sour cream into a small container. Stir the ground cumin into the sour cream.

While the fish is marinating, assemble the zesty cabbage slaw by simply mixing all the ingredients together.

Fry the marinated fish, skin side down, in a large frying pan on high heat. As soon as the fish starts to turn solid white, turn it over and cook for another 4–5 minutes. Flake the fish fillets and check for any hidden bones.

To assemble the tacos, start by adding some cabbage slaw to the taco shell, followed by some flaked fish and a few avo slices. Top with a spoonful of spiced sour cream.

Yields 6 tacos

Loaded beef nachos (Mexico)

THESE ARE GREAT WITH DIPS AND ARE ESPECIALLY FILLING AS A FUN FAMILY MEAL.

RECIPE	PORTIONS	TOTAL CARBS	FIBRE	NET CARBS	FAT	PROTEIN	KJ
Beef nachos	1	23 g	13.5 g	9.5 g	39 g	42 g	2 500

NACHOS

1 quantity Dough 2, made with
1 cup sunflower seed flour + 1 cup
golden or brown flax meal (p. 17)
1 tsp salt
½ tsp paprika
¼ tsp chilli flakes (optional)
½ tsp onion flakes (optional)
¼ tsp garlic flakes (optional)

BEEF AND TOPPINGS

500 g beef mince
2 Tbsp coconut oil
½ tsp each ground cumin, paprika,
crushed garlic, salt and pepper
1 tsp BBQ spice (sugar-free)
2 Tbsp tomato paste
2 Tbsp xylitol
1 cup cherry tomatoes, chopped
3–4 spring onions, sliced
Sliced chillies (optional)
1 handful fresh chives, chopped
½ cup thick sour cream or crème
fraîche (optional)
2 cups grated cheese (Cheddar or a
mix of Cheddar and mozzarella)
1 avocado, cubed (optional)

Preheat the oven to 180 °C. Line a baking sheet with baking paper.

Prepare the dough as described in the recipe, adding the spices to the dry ingredients before adding it to the butter-water mixture.

Line a large chopping board or flat surface with plastic wrap and use a rolling pin to roll out the chilled dough into a rectangle 2–3 mm thick (see Lekker Tip below). Using a 14 cm (or there about) ramekin or smaller cereal bowl, cut out circles from the dough. Form another ball with the offcut pieces and repeat the process until you have used all of the dough. You need eight circles for this recipe.

Use the bottom layer of plastic wrap as a support to lift and peel off the circles and place them onto the baking sheet. Now cut each circle as you would a pizza so that you have eight triangles per round.

Bake for 15–20 minutes or until crisp and slightly browned. Allow to cool slightly, then break each round into nacho triangles on the previously cut lines. Give a quick grind of salt to taste.

In a heavy-bottomed saucepan on medium to high heat, brown the beef in coconut oil for 2–3 minutes. Add the spices, tomato paste and xylitol. Allow to infuse and cook on medium heat for 3–4 minutes, stirring occasionally. You want the meat to have slightly saucy clusters but generally be on the dry side.

Preheat the oven to 200 °C.

In an ovenproof dish, add a layer using half of the nachos followed by half of the beef. Add more layers using half of the tomatoes, onions, chillies, chives, sour cream and cheese. Repeat all the layers, making sure to end with a layer of grated cheese. Bake for 6–8 minutes or until the cheese is melted. Top with avo and a grind of salt and black pepper.

Serve immediately.

Yields 4–6 portions

LEKKER TIP

It is sometimes helpful to place another piece of plastic wrap on top of the dough and roll on the plastic wrap rather than the actual dough.

Chicken quesadilla (Mexico)

SERVE WITH A FIBRE-FILLED GREEN SALAD AND PREPARE TO SMILE!

RECIPE	PORTIONS	TOTAL CARBS	FIBRE	NET CARBS	FAT	PROTEIN	KJ
Chicken quesadilla	1	33 g	21 g	12 g	49.9 g	36.3 g	3 000

QUESADILLA

2 quantities Dough 2 (p. 17) –
works really well with 2 cups
sunflower seed flour as a base or
substitute with 1 cup nut flour to
lower carb count)

FILLING

2 chicken breast fillets, cut into
thin strips
1 red pepper, sliced into thin strips
1 tsp crushed garlic
¼ tsp each chilli flakes, coriander,
ground cumin and paprika
2 Tbsp coconut oil
Salt and pepper to taste
1 x 250 g tub crème fraîche
4 spring onions, sliced
2 cups grated cheese of choice

Preheat the oven to 180 °C.

Prepare a double batch of dough as described in the recipe. Divide the chilled dough ball into four equal portions. Place each portion on its own sheet of baking paper and use a rolling pin to roll them into circles 4–5 mm thick.

Bake for 15 minutes or until the base no longer sticks to the paper. Remove from oven, but leave the oven switched on. Flip two of the bases over on the baking paper so the bottoms now face up and place the paper and bases on two baking sheets.

In a frying pan on medium to high heat, stir-fry the chicken, red pepper, garlic and spices in coconut oil. Add salt and pepper to taste.

Spread half the crème fraîche onto the two bottom bases. Top with the stir-fry mixture, spring onions and cheese, sandwich with the remaining two bases and bake until the cheese starts to melt.

Cut into pizza-like slices and enjoy hot!

Yields 2 stuffed quesadillas, which should satisfy 4–6 enthusiastic diners

Sushi (Japan)

ALL-YOU-CAN-EAT SUSHI BUFFETS USED TO BE MY HUSBAND'S HAPPY PLACE BEFORE LOW CARB ENTERED OUR LIVES. SINCE THEN, I'VE REPLACED THE SUGAR-SPIKING INGREDIENTS WITH HEALTHY FATS AND FIBRE GALORE TO BRING THIS BELOVED FARE BACK TO OUR TABLE. YOU CAN ASSEMBLE IT IN NO TIME AND EVEN MY SON, WHO DOES NOT EAT CABBAGE, DEVOURS BOTH VERSIONS! SERVE WITH THE QUICK ASIAN SALAD (P. 121) MADE WITHOUT THE STEAK.

RECIPE	PORTIONS	TOTAL CARBS	FIBRE	NET CARBS	FAT	PROTEIN	KJ
Sushi option 1	1 piece	6.8 g	4.6 g	2.2 g	7 g	3.2 g	380
Sushi option 2	1 piece	9.3 g	6.1 g	3.2 g	7 g	3.2 g	412

OPTION 1

2 Tbsp coconut oil
300 g grated cauliflower
1 Tbsp xylitol
Pinch salt
1 Tbsp psyllium husk powder
1 Tbsp apple cider vinegar
3 Tbsp sunflower seed flour

OPTION 2

2 Tbsp coconut oil
500 g cabbage, finely grated
1 Tbsp xylitol
Pinch salt
3 Tbsp water
1½ Tbsp psyllium husk powder
1 Tbsp apple cider vinegar
3 Tbsp sunflower seed flour

TO ASSEMBLE AND SERVE

2 sheets nori
Finely julienned cucumber (deseeded), carrots and spring onion
Thin slices avocado, salmon, tuna or cream cheese
Wasabi (optional)
Soy sauce (optional)

For option 1, add the coconut oil to a heavy-bottomed pan on medium heat and let it warm up before adding the cauliflower, xylitol and salt. Sauté until just starting to soften. Turn the heat down if necessary.

Place the warm sautéed cauli crumbles into a blender or food processor along with the psyllium husk powder, vinegar and sunflower seed flour. Blend for a few seconds until well combined. It will form an almost sticky dough. Divide the 'rice' dough into two equal portions.

For option 2, add the coconut oil to a heavy-bottomed pan on medium heat and let it warm up before adding the cabbage, xylitol and salt. Sauté the cabbage until soft. Add the water to steam the cabbage a bit. Turn the heat down if necessary.

Place the warm sautéed cabbage into a blender or food processor along with the psyllium husk powder, vinegar and sunflower seed flour and blend for a few seconds until well combined. It will form an almost sticky dough. Divide the 'rice' dough into two equal portions.

To assemble the sushi, lay out one sheet of nori on a plastic wrap-covered bamboo mat. Start working the 'rice' dough into a thin layer over most of the sheet. Take some cucumber and carrot strips and lay them on top. Add slices of your chosen filling next to the julienned veggies. Roll up on the bamboo mat, compact and roll. Repeat the process. Refrigerate until firmed up before you cut each roll into 6–8 pieces. Serve with wasabi and soy sauce.

Yields 12 sushi pieces

Orange chicken on baby marrow noodles (China)

RECIPE	PORTIONS	TOTAL CARBS	FIBRE	NET CARBS	FAT	PROTEIN	KJ
Orange chicken	1	27.6 g	5.4 g	23.2 g	22.6 g	47.2 g	1 976

CHICKEN
4–5 eggs
8 Tbsp coconut flour
Salt and pepper to taste
4 chicken breast fillets, cubed
¼ cup coconut oil
2 cups julienned peppers
2 spring onions, sliced
Black sesame seeds (optional)

SAUCE
3 Tbsp soy sauce
1 Tbsp xylitol
Juice and zest of 1 orange
1 Tbsp grated fresh ginger or 1 tsp ground ginger
1 tsp crushed garlic
1 Tbsp apple cider vinegar
½ tsp chilli flakes
Salt and pepper to taste

BABY MARROW NOODLES
12 medium to large baby marrows, sliced into ribbons with a vegetable peeler
Coconut oil for frying
Pinch salt

For the chicken, whisk the eggs in a mixing bowl. Mix the coconut flour and seasoning together in a deep dish plate. In batches, dip the chicken pieces into the egg, then the flour and then the egg again.

In a separate bowl, mix all the sauce ingredients together until the xylitol has dissolved.

Heat the coconut oil in a heavy-bottomed pan on medium heat, and then add the double-dipped chicken nuggets. Fry for 2–3 minutes on each side or until golden brown. Remove from the pan and set aside.

As soon as all the nuggets are done, or in a separate pan with a bit of coconut oil, stir-fry the peppers. Return the nuggets to the pan and add the sauce and spring onions. Allow the sauce to simmer, thicken and infuse into the nuggets. Even though it is not a lot of sauce, it reduces fairly quickly and gives the nuggets a lovely, slightly sticky coating.

To make the noodles, stir-fry the baby marrows in a little coconut oil for 2–3 minutes, making sure they stay on the crunchier side. Add the salt.

Pile the baby marrows into four bowls and top with the saucy nuggets and peppers. Sprinkle with black sesame seeds.

Yields 4 portions

Sesame chicken on egg fried cauli rice
(China)

RECIPE	PORTIONS	TOTAL CARBS	FIBRE	NET CARBS	FAT	PROTEIN	KJ
Sesame chicken	1	15.5 g	5.6 g	9.9 g	20.5 g	45.1 g	1 672

SESAME CHICKEN

4–5 deboned chicken breasts, skin on, chopped into bite-size pieces

4 Tbsp coconut oil or lard

Salt and pepper

1 tsp crushed garlic

1 heaped tsp Thai seven spice mix

½ tsp ground cinnamon

½ tsp ground ginger

¼ tsp chilli flakes (optional)

¼ cup vinegar of choice

2 Tbsp soy sauce

4 Tbsp xylitol

½ cup water

4–5 spring onions, roughly chopped

1 x 250 g punnet mushrooms, sliced

1 red pepper, chopped

350 g broccoli florets, halved

3 Tbsp sesame seeds (regular and/or black)

EGG FRIED CAULI RICE

1 large head cauliflower, made into cauli rice in a food processor

2 Tbsp coconut oil or lard

Pinch salt

4 eggs, whisked briefly

Start with the chicken. In a pan on medium to high heat, brown the chicken pieces in 2 Tbsp of the coconut oil for a few minutes. Add salt and pepper to taste. Stir in the garlic, spices, vinegar, soy sauce and xylitol. Add the water and allow to simmer and reduce a bit. (Add a bit more water if needed.)

In a separate pan, brown the spring onions and the rest of the chopped veggies in the remaining coconut oil on medium heat for 1–3 minutes. The veggies should remain crunchy. Add to the simmering chicken pieces and stir the sesame seeds into the dish.

While the chicken is simmering, make the cauli rice. In a heavy-bottomed pan over high heat, stir-fry the cauli rice briefly in the coconut oil. Add salt. Pour the whisked eggs into the centre of the pan and allow it to cook a bit before stirring gently – don't overwork the rice mix. Remove from heat as soon as the egg is cooked through the cauli rice.

Spoon the cauli rice into bowls and top with the sesame chicken.

Yields 4–5 portions

Lamb rogan josh with garlic flatbread (India)

RECIPE	PORTIONS	TOTAL CARBS	FIBRE	NET CARBS	FAT	PROTEIN	KJ
Lamb rogan josh	1	17 g	6.3 g	11.7 g	38 g	5 g	2 424
Garlic flatbread	1 flatbread	11 g	6 g	5 g	13 g	5 g	710

LAMB ROGAN JOSH
1–1.2 kg stewing lamb
3 Tbsp coconut oil for frying
1 medium red onion, chopped
2 tsp crushed garlic
2 tsp chopped fresh ginger
1 cup water or bone broth
1 x 400 g can chopped tomatoes in juice
2 Tbsp xylitol
8 baby marrows chopped
2 medium brinjals, diced
400 g pumpkin, diced
½ x 400 ml can coconut cream or 1 cup double-cream plain yoghurt
Fresh coriander leaves for garnishing

HOME-MADE SPICE BLEND
½ tsp each ground cumin, ground coriander, chilli flakes, fennel seeds, ground cardamom and ground cloves
1 tsp each ground cinnamon, salt, curry powder and black peppercorns

GARLIC FLATBREAD
1 quantity Dough 1, without optional cheese (p. 14)
Coconut oil or butter for frying
1–2 Tbsp crushed garlic
50 g butter, melted
Salt and pepper to taste

Start with the rogan josh. In a heavy-bottomed saucepan on medium-high heat, brown the lamb in the coconut oil for 5–6 minutes. Add the Home-made Spice Blend, onion, garlic and ginger. Allow the flavours to develop and form a thick coating around the meat. Add the water to loosen the layer of spices and meat from the base of the saucepan.

In a slow-cooker set on high, add the spicy lamb and liquid, the tomatoes and xylitol and cook for 4 hours or more before adding the veggies. Cook for another 1–2 hours.

Using a slotted spoon, transfer the meat and veggies from the slow-cooker to a saucepan on medium heat. Add 1 cup of the cooking liquid from the slow-cooker to the saucepan, along with half of the coconut cream. Cook for 5 minutes and allow the sauce to reduce and thicken. Spoon into a bowl, add some of the remaining coconut cream as a garnish and top with fresh coriander leaves.

To make the flatbreads, prepare the dough as described in the recipe. Divide the chilled dough ball into six equal portions. On a plastic wrap-covered chopping board, roll each portion into a 3–4 mm-thick circle. Heat a pan on medium to medium-high heat. Add the coconut oil and allow to warm up a bit before gently lifting the plastic wrap from the chopping board and peeling off the flatbread dough. Add one flatbread at a time to the prepared pan. Fry for 2 minutes on each side or until a few lovely brown cooking spots appear. These flatbreads soak up the oil quite a bit so be sure to add about 2 Tbsp coconut oil before frying each flatbread. In a separate bowl, mix the garlic and melted butter and brush onto each flatbread. Season to taste and serve with the rogan josh.

Yields 6 portions rogan josh and 6 flatbreads

Old-fashioned Cornish pies (England)

RECIPE	PORTIONS	TOTAL CARBS	FIBRE	NET CARBS	FAT	PROTEIN	KJ
Cornish pies	1 pie	17.9 g	8.7 g	9.2 g	19.3 g	29.3 g	1 470

MEAT FILLING

500–600 g beef mince, beef cubes or stewing beef, deboned and cubed

1 medium onion, finely chopped

½ tsp crushed garlic

3 Tbsp butter or coconut oil

1 cup shredded cabbage

1 cup chopped green beans

1 medium carrot, chopped

1 cup diced pumpkin

Small handful fresh parsley, chopped

½ Tbsp chopped fresh rosemary

½ Tbsp chopped fresh thyme

¼–½ cup water

Salt and black pepper to taste

PIE 'PASTRY'

1½ quantities Dough 1, without optional cheese (p. 14)

1 egg, beaten

Salt to taste

For the filling, brown the meat, onion and garlic in the coconut oil in a heavy-bottomed saucepan on medium to high heat for 5–8 minutes. Stir often to ensure the meat is evenly browned. Add the veggies, herbs, water and seasoning, lower the heat to medium and simmer with the lid on for another 5–8 minutes. Remove the lid and simmer for a further 3 minutes. The filling should have a thick, saucy consistency. Remove from heat and allow to cool.

Preheat the oven to 180 °C. Line a baking sheet with baking paper.

Prepare the dough as described in the recipe. Line a large chopping board or flat surface with plastic wrap and roll out the chilled dough into a 5 mm-thick rectangle. Use a saucer to cut out circles from the dough. Gather the offcuts together and roll again. You need eight circles for this recipe.

Add one serving spoon of meat filling in the middle of each dough circle. Tuck your hand under the plastic wrap and use it as a support to lift the sides of the dough over the meat filling. You want the two sides to meet in the middle. Start on the one side and gently pinch and turn the dough around the filling. It should look rustic and almost like a dinosaur's back. Gently lift the pies from the plastic wrap and place onto the prepared baking sheet. Brush with beaten egg and finish with a good grind of salt.

Bake for 25–30 minutes.

Yields 8 pies

LEKKER TIP

Freeze the pies before baking for those days when you're pressed for time.

Under
30-minute
meals

Mild butter chicken served with garlic and herb flatbread

RECIPE	PORTIONS	TOTAL CARBS	FIBRE	NET CARBS	FAT	PROTEIN	KJ
Mild butter chicken	1	6.9 g	1.8 g	5.1 g	25.5 g	50 g	2 104
Flatbread	1 flatbread	11 g	6 g	5 g	13 g	5 g	710

SPICE BLEND

¼ tsp each cayenne pepper, ground coriander, ground cardamom, fennel seeds
½ tsp each cumin seeds, black pepper, salt, ground cinnamon
Pinch ground cloves
1 tsp curry powder
2 tsp paprika
2 Tbsp xylitol

GARLIC AND HERB FLATBREAD

1 quantity Dough 1, without optional cheese (p. 14)
1–2 Tbsp finely chopped fresh herbs of choice
1 Tbsp garlic
Sea or Himalayan salt to taste
Grind of pepper to taste
Coconut oil or butter for frying

CHICKEN

1–1.2 kg chicken pieces
2 Tbsp coconut oil for frying
1 x 400 g can whole peeled tomatoes in juice (keep the can to measure the water)
1 Tbsp grated fresh ginger
1 Tbsp crushed garlic
½ x 400 ml can coconut cream or ¾ cup fresh cream

GARNISH (OPTIONAL)

½ cup double-cream plain yoghurt or crème fraîche
Roughly chopped fresh coriander leaves

Mix all the spice blend ingredients together and set aside.

For the flatbreads, follow the steps to make dough 1 as described in the dough method. Add the herbs and salt and pepper to taste into the dry ingredients before adding it to the butter and water mixture. Follow the rest of the steps as described. Take your chilled dough ball and divide into six equal parts. On a cling wrap-covered chopping board, roll each part into a 3–4 mm-thick circular shape, almost like a mini pizza. Heat a pan on medium to medium-high heat. Add your oil or butter and allow to warm up a bit before gently lifting the cling wrap from the chopping board and peeling off the flatbread dough, adding one flatbread at a time to the prepared pan. Fry for 2 minutes on each side or until a few lovely brown cooking spots appear. These flatbreads soak up the oil quite a bit so be sure to top up about 2 Tbsp coconut oil or butter before each new flatbread.

In a heavy-bottomed saucepan on medium heat, brown the chicken pieces in the coconut oil for 8–10 minutes. Remove from the saucepan and allow to cool in order to debone them.

In the same saucepan, add the spice blend and stir for 1 minute to allow the flavours to develop. Add the tomatoes, ginger, garlic, cream and a canful of water to the spices and simmer for 10 minutes on low heat. Add the deboned chicken and simmer for another 5–7 minutes.

Garnish with yoghurt and coriander leaves and serve with the flatbreads to soak up the sauce.

Yields 6–8 portions butter chicken and 6 flatbreads

> **LEKKER TIP**
> By deboning the chicken pieces yourself, you tend to get juicier, fattier meat and you're left with bones for making bone broth. But if you're short on time, use chicken breast fillets instead.

Quick green bean and beef stew

RECIPE	PORTIONS	TOTAL CARBS	FIBRE	NET CARBS	FAT	PROTEIN	KJ
Green bean stew	1	18.4 g	6.8 g	11.6 g	17 g	40 g	1 528

600–800 g beef strips, beef stir-fry or minute steaks (I mostly use leftover Sunday roast that I cut into strips)
50 g butter
1 Tbsp BBQ spice (sugar-free)
Salt and black pepper
700 g fresh green beans, topped and tailed
6–8 small baby marrows, julienned
¼–½ tsp crushed garlic
Generous handful chopped fresh herbs (chives, thyme, oregano)
½ cup frozen peas
1 cup fresh cream or coconut cream
1 cup grated Cheddar cheese

If you are not using leftover roast beef, give the meat a quick stir-fry in a frying pan on medium to high heat, using half the butter, the BBQ spice, and salt and pepper to taste. Transfer the cooked beef into a separate dish and allow to rest for a few minutes.

In the same pan, add the rest of the butter and let it infuse into the meaty pan juices. Sauté the green beans, baby marrows, garlic and herbs for 4–5 minutes or until slightly softened. Add the frozen peas and cream and let the dish simmer and thicken for 3–4 minutes on low to medium heat. Return the beef to the pan and heat through. Serve in a deep bowl, topped with a grind of black pepper and some grated cheese.

Yields 4–6 portions

Chicken schnitzel

RECIPE	PORTIONS	TOTAL CARBS	FIBRE	NET CARBS	FAT	PROTEIN	KJ
Chicken schnitzel	1 schnitzel	2.5 g	1.1 g	1.4 g	32 g	44 g	1 912

4 deboned chicken breasts (or use pork or tenderised steak)
3–4 eggs
6–8 Tbsp coconut flour
2 Tbsp grated Parmesan cheese
1 Tbsp chopped fresh thyme, chives or oregano or a combination
Salt and pepper to taste
¼ cup coconut oil for frying

Flatten the chicken breasts into schnitzels using a meat mallet.

Whisk the eggs in a mixing bowl. In a deep dish plate, mix the coconut flour, Parmesan, herbs and seasoning. In batches, dip the chicken schnitzels into the egg, then the flour and then the egg again.

Heat the coconut oil in a heavy-bottomed pan on medium heat, and then add a double-dipped schnitzel. Fry for 3–4 minutes on each side or until golden brown and crispy. Repeat with the rest of the schnitzels. Serve with any side or salad (pp. 117–133).

Yields 4 schnitzels

Italian more-than-meatballs casserole

THIS CASSEROLE SMELLS LIKE FRESHLY BAKED PIZZA AND IS PERFECT FOR ENTERTAINING. IT IS ONE OF THOSE MEMORABLE, EASY DISHES THAT WILL WIN A SPOT ON THE WEEKLY MENU.

RECIPE	PORTIONS	TOTAL CARBS	FIBRE	NET CARBS	FAT	PROTEIN	KJ
Meatball casserole	1	12.5 g	4.5 g	8 g	19 g	48 g	1 628

1 kg beef mince (preferably not lean)
1 egg
¼ cup chopped fresh parsley
Zest of 1 lemon
Salt and black pepper to taste
3 Tbsp coconut oil
1 kg baby marrows, quartered lengthways
2 x 400 g cans whole cherry tomatoes in juice
2 Tbsp xylitol
2 tsp crushed garlic
2–3 Tbsp chopped fresh oregano, thyme and rosemary (or 1½ tsp dried Italian herbs)
½ cup olives, pitted (optional – not always enjoyed by kids)
1 cup cubed mozzarella cheese (or more to preference)
1 x 300 g bag baby spinach
Grated Parmesan cheese and chopped fresh herbs for garnishing (optional)

Preheat the oven to 190 °C.

Mix the beef mince, egg, parsley, lemon zest, salt and pepper together in a mixing bowl and roll into medium-sized meatballs.

In a Dutch oven or ovenproof saucepan on medium-high heat, brown the meatballs in the coconut oil. Remove the meatballs from the pan and set aside.

Sauté the baby marrows in the pan juices for 3–4 minutes.

Spread out the baby marrows into an even layer. Top with 1 can of tomatoes. Sprinkle 1 Tbsp xylitol, 1 tsp garlic, 1 Tbsp herbs, a few olives and half of the cheese. Next, pack in a layer of spinach and then arrange the meatballs on top. Add the remaining can of tomatoes followed by the remaining xylitol, garlic, herbs, olives and cheese.

Bake with the lid on for 25 minutes and then grill, lid off, for 5 minutes. Serve in a deep dish with a plain green salad and vinaigrette on the side. Or give it some real entertainment status by adding Garlic, Cheese, Herb and Olive Focaccia (p. 92) to dip into the fragrant sauce.

Garnish with grated Parmesan and chopped fresh herbs.

Yields 6–8 portions

LEKKER TIP
Use any leftovers to make a lovely lunchtime soup for one or two. Simply remove the meatballs and blend the veggies into the sauce. Add a dash of cream or coconut milk, crumble the meatballs back into the soup and Koos is your cousin!

Quizza (Quiche pizza)

RECIPE	PORTIONS	TOTAL CARBS	FIBRE	NET CARBS	FAT	PROTEIN	KJ
Quizza	1 quarter	8.6 g	2 g	6.6 g	23.2 g	19.7 g	1 252
Quizza	1 eighth	4.3 g	1 g	3.3 g	11.6 g	9.8 g	624

BASE
4 eggs
¼ cup cream cheese
1 Tbsp coconut oil for frying
3 medium baby marrows, roughly grated
Salt

TOPPING
2 Tbsp tomato purée
3–4 slices good quality salami
Generous handful grated cheese (mozzarella or white Cheddar)
Grind of your favourite salt or herbed salt

Preheat the oven grill.

For the base, blend the eggs and cream cheese together using a hand blender until it has a creamy consistency.

In a medium to large ovenproof pan on medium to high heat, melt the coconut oil and spread the grated baby marrows over the surface of the pan. Sprinkle with salt and fry for 1 minute without stirring. Now add the cream cheese mixture and allow the batter to form a crust and set on the sides of the pan only – about 2 minutes.

Pop the pan into the oven under the grill. The quizza base will get puffy and will brown within 3–4 minutes.

Take out of the oven and spread with the tomato purée. Add the salami (or a veggie topping) and the cheese. Grind over salt. Pop back into the oven for another 2–3 minutes.

Cut into your preferred portion sizes and enjoy.

Yields 4 quarters or 8 smaller portions

Fragrant hake kebabs

RECIPE	PORTIONS	TOTAL CARBS	FIBRE	NET CARBS	FAT	PROTEIN	KJ
Hake kebabs	1	4.8 g	1.5 g	3.3 g	33 g	31 g	1 736

600 g hake fillets, skin removed
and cubed
6 fresh asparagus spears, cut into
3 pieces each (or use baby marrow
if asparagus is not in season)
Butter or coconut oil for frying
½ red pepper, cubed
12 olives, pitted

BASTING SAUCE
3 Tbsp butter
2 Tbsp lemon juice
2 tsp crushed garlic
1 tsp curry powder
1 Tbsp chopped fresh mixed herbs
or 1 tsp dried mixed herbs
1 tsp xylitol (optional)
4 Tbsp double-cream plain yoghurt
½ tsp Dijon mustard
Salt and pepper to taste

For the marinade, melt the butter in a saucepan on low heat, and then add the rest of the marinade ingredients. Allow the flavours to infuse for a minute or two. Remove from heat and allow to cool.

Pour the marinade over the hake pieces and marinate for 5 minutes. Meanwhile, quickly sauté the asparagus in butter or coconut oil.

Assemble the kebabs by threading alternating cubes of fish, red pepper and olives onto skewers. Fry in a pan with 2 Tbsp coconut oil on medium heat for 2–3 minutes each side, turning twice.

Serve with the Retro Cucumber and Avo Ring (p. 133).

Yields 4–6 portions

Pesto-butter steak strips

THIS RECIPE IS SO EASY AND IT HAS A GREAT BALANCE BETWEEN HEALTHY FATS, EXCELLENT PROTEIN AND FIBRE.

RECIPE	PORTIONS	TOTAL CARBS	FIBRE	NET CARBS	FAT	PROTEIN	KJ
Steak strips	1	14.2 g	6.2 g	8 g	41 g	59 g	2 656

4 Tbsp melted coconut oil
600–700 g steak (use the cut of your choice)
2 Tbsp meat rub, BBQ spice or salt and pepper
350 g fresh green beans
100 g asparagus
400 g tenderstem broccoli
Coconut oil for frying
Good grind of herbed salt and pepper to taste
Squeeze of lemon juice
100 g butter, room temperature
1 Tbsp basil or any other pesto
½ tsp crushed garlic (or to taste)

Rub the coconut oil into the steak and apply the meat rub, spice or seasoning. In a frying pan on high heat, cook the steak until done to your liking, turning only once or twice. Allow the steak to rest on a chopping board for a few minutes.

In the same pan on medium heat, stir-fry the veggies in the steak pan juices, only adding more healthy fats if the pan juices are not enough. Stir-fry for 5–6 minutes. Season to taste with herbed salt, pepper and lemon juice.

Mix the butter, pesto and garlic together.

Cut the steak into diagonal strips. Dish some veggies onto plates, add the steak strips and top with a spoonful of pesto and garlic butter.

Yields 4–6 satisfying portions

> **LEKKER TIP**
> The steak can also be cooked on the braai.

Lamb lollies with minted pea purée

SERVE WITH A SALAD OR SMOKY BRINJAL CHIPS.

RECIPE	PORTIONS	TOTAL CARBS	FIBRE	NET CARBS	FAT	PROTEIN	KJ
Lamb lollies	1	22 g	11.6 g	10.4 g	30 g	44.2 g	2 104

SMOKY BRINJAL CHIPS
2 medium brinjals
¼ cup melted coconut oil or butter
2 Tbsp BBQ spice (sugar free)
1 tsp garlic salt
1 tsp paprika
1 Tbsp chopped fresh rosemary
(optional)

LAMB LOLLIES
500 g lamb mince
1 tsp paprika
1 tsp crushed garlic
2 spring onions, thinly sliced
2 Tbsp chopped fresh parsley
1 Tbsp chopped fresh rosemary
(optional)
½ Tbsp chopped fresh mint
(optional)
1 egg
100 g feta cheese (individually-
wrapped block cut into 6–8 strips)
6–8 medium kebab sticks

MINTED PEA PURÉE
½ cup minted peas
2 cm-thick cucumber round
1 Tbsp water
Salt and pepper to taste

If you are serving the lamb lollies with brinjal chips, start with these first or move on to the next component if you are having it with a salad.

Preheat the oven to 200 °C. Line one or two baking sheets with baking paper.

Wash and slice the brinjals as thinly as possible – no more than 5 mm thick. Place on the baking sheet(s) and brush the melted coconut oil on both sides. Sprinkle the herbs and spices on both sides. Bake for about 20 minutes, turning once or twice, until crispy.

For the lamb lollies, place all the ingredients, except the feta cheese, in a bowl and mix well. Thread a feta strip onto one end of a skewer and then press and shape small amounts of the mince mixture around the cheese. Repeat with the rest of the ingredients. In a frying pan on medium heat, fry the lamb lollies for about 10 minutes, turning often so that it is evenly browned all over.

For the pea purée, blend all the ingredients together in a blender for 10–20 seconds or until the purée has a very smooth consistency.

Put all the elements together and add your personal serving flare!

Yields 3–4 portions

Chilli in a jiffy

THIS SAUCY CHILLI IS THE MEXICAN COUSIN OF OUR GOOD OLD 'CURRY AND RICE'. IT IS SO FLAVOURFUL AND FILLING, AND THE INTENSITY OF THE CHILLI CAN EASILY BE ADJUSTED TO YOUR PREFERENCE. COMBINE WITH FRESH CHILLIES FOR A DECENT BURN OR OMIT THEM ALTOGETHER TO MAKE A SAVOURY MINCE INSTEAD.

RECIPE	PORTIONS	TOTAL CARBS	FIBRE	NET CARBS	FAT	PROTEIN	KJ
Chilli in a jiffy	1	16.8 g	7 g	9.8 g	17.8 g	51 g	1 724

Coconut oil for frying
1 small to medium red onion, diced
1 red pepper, deseeded and cubed
1 brinjal, diced into 1 cm cubes
2 cups roughly chopped cauliflower
500 g beef mince
500 g pork mince
1 tsp crushed garlic
1 tsp ground coriander
1 tsp ground cumin
Chilli flakes to taste (I use ½ tsp)
1 Tbsp BBQ spice (sugar free) or salt and pepper to taste
2 Tbsp chopped fresh mixed herbs or 1 tsp dried mixed herbs
2 Tbsp xylitol
1 cup sliced green beans
½ cup peas
1–2 x 400 g cans chopped tomatoes in juice

In a heavy-bottomed saucepan on medium to high heat, use a few tablespoons of coconut oil to sauté the onion, red pepper, brinjal and cauliflower for 4–5 minutes until soft. Remove from the pan and set aside.

Add more coconut oil to the saucepan if needed. Add the meat and start to brown. As soon as the meat starts to brown, add the rest of the ingredients, including the onion and red pepper mixture. Turn the heat down to medium and allow to simmer gently for 10–15 minutes. Stir occasionally and check the seasoning.

Scoop into deep bowls, top with a dollop of sour cream and serve with a spoon. Alternatively, add a flatbread (pp. 57, 61), scoop onto a savoury waffle (p. 73), serve over nachos (p. 50), stuff a taco (p. 49), fill an omelette and add some cheese, or even allow to cool a bit and serve in lettuce cups with a slice of avo, some salsa and a dollop of sour cream.

Yields 4–6 portions

LEKKER TIPS
- This recipe will stretch into more servings depending on what you are serving with the chilli.
- Choose your saucy consistency by using either 2 cans of tomatoes for a very saucy, almost stew-like dish or use 1 can for a thicker consistency that is perfect for a taco filling, roti or savoury waffle. You are welcome to substitute the pork with more beef, but the mix lends a great flavour.

Creamy chicken carbonara

RECIPE	PORTIONS	TOTAL CARBS	FIBRE	NET CARBS	FAT	PROTEIN	KJ
Chicken carbonara	1	12.3 g	3 g	9.3 g	33 g	33 g	1 876

4 Tbsp coconut oil for frying
3–4 chicken breast fillets, sliced into strips
4 rashers bacon, sliced into 5–6 pieces each
1 cup sliced peppers
3 cups sliced mushrooms
1–2 tsp crushed garlic
1 cup fresh cream
1 cup sour cream
2 eggs plus 2 egg yolks, whisked
4 Tbsp grated Parmesan or 1 cup grated Cheddar cheese
1–2 Tbsp fresh thyme
1 kg baby marrows, sliced into ribbons
1 Tbsp snipped fresh chives to sprinkle on top (optional)
1–2 spring onions, thinly sliced
Pinch ground nutmeg (optional)
Salt and black pepper to taste

In a frying pan on medium high heat, add 2 Tbsp of the coconut oil and chicken and fry until almost fully cooked. Add the bacon pieces, peppers, mushrooms and garlic and cook for a further 3–4 minutes.

Add the cream and sour cream and simmer for 5–6 minutes. While stirring, add the whisked eggs and yolks, cheese and thyme. Continue stirring until all the cheese is melted through.

In a separate pan on medium to high heat, add the remaining 2 Tbsp coconut oil and stir-fry the baby marrow ribbons until just tender but not soggy. Pile the cooked veggie ribbons onto serving plates and scoop a generous amount of carbonara over the noodles. Garnish with chives, spring onions, a pinch ground nutmeg and a generous grind of salt and black pepper to taste.

Yields 4–6 portions

Savoury waffle sloppy joes

THIS IS ANOTHER GEM THAT I PICKED UP IN THE USA – EASY, LAID-BACK COOKING THAT IS ABSOLUTELY SATISFYING.

RECIPE	PORTIONS	TOTAL CARBS	FIBRE	NET CARBS	FAT	PROTEIN	KJ
Sloppy joes	1	9.8 g	4.5 g	5.3 g	33 g	42 g	2 640

½ quantity Baby Marrow
Bolognaise (p. 41)
1 quantity Dough 7 (p. 28) – any
savoury option
4–6 eggs (optional)
1 cup grated Cheddar cheese
(optional)

Prepare the bolognaise sauce according to the recipe.

While the meat is simmering, turn on your waffle pan and prepare the waffle batter. Bake the waffles and, as soon as you have the last waffles in the pan, fry some sunny side-up eggs.

Assemble the sloppy joes – waffle, meat, cheese and egg. Serve with a side salad or veggie slices if desired, although I find this fibre-filled dish very filling on its own.

Yields 4–6 portions

LEKKER TIP
I make my waffles round even though I bake them in a square waffle iron. It looks pretty with the round egg on top and yields more waffles this way.

Batter-fried fish and sweet potato fries

I'VE ONLY INCLUDED TWO RECIPES USING SWEET POTATO – THIS ONE ABSOLUTELY NEEDS A SWEET POTATO TO BE COMPLETE.
PLEASE DON'T EAT SWEET POTATO CHIPS WITH EVERY MEAL – THEY ARE VERY HIGH IN CARBS AND VERY EASY TO OVEREAT
SO I SUGGEST SERVING THIS WITH A LARGE SALAD PORTION AND A SMALLER PORTION OF CHIPS.

RECIPE	PORTIONS	TOTAL CARBS	FIBRE	NET CARBS	FAT	PROTEIN	KJ
Batter-fried fish	1	22.8 g	4 g	18.8 g	42 g	31 g	2 348

SWEET POTATO CHIPS
4 medium sweet potatoes, skin on, scrubbed, cut into chips
¼ cup coconut oil for baking
Salt to taste
Pinch paprika

BATTER-FRIED FISH
3–4 eggs
6–8 Tbsp coconut flour
1–2 tsp fish seasoning spices
Salt and white pepper to taste
4–6 hake fillets
¼ cup coconut oil for frying fish

Preheat the oven to 200 °C. Line a baking sheet with baking paper.

Place the sweet potato chips in a bag with the coconut oil and give it a shake until the chips are evenly coated in oil. Spread the chips out over the prepared baking sheet(s) and sprinkle with salt and paprika. Bake for 20 minutes until crispy and brown, turning halfway through.

Whisk the eggs in a mixing bowl. Mix the coconut flour, fish seasoning, salt and pepper in a deep dish plate. In batches, dip the hake into the egg, then the flour and then the egg again.

Heat a large heavy-bottomed pan with coconut oil to medium-high heat. Pan-fry two hake fillets, skin side down, for 3–5 minutes or until golden brown. Turn over the hake and fry for another 3–4 minutes or until the fish flakes easily. Serve with a lovely green salad and a small portion of the sweet potato chips.

Yields 4–6 portions

Chicken curry on coconut cauli mash

RECIPE	PORTIONS	TOTAL CARBS	FIBRE	NET CARBS	FAT	PROTEIN	KJ
Chicken curry	1	23 g	9.4 g	13.6 g	38.2 g	43 g	2 368

CHICKEN CURRY

2 cups cubed brinjal
1 medium onion, diced
1 cup diced mixed red and yellow peppers
2 Tbsp coconut oil for frying
4 chicken breast fillets, cubed
1 tsp crushed garlic
1 tsp grated fresh ginger
1 x 400 ml can coconut cream
½ cup peas
1 Tbsp mild and flavoursome curry powder
Salt and black pepper to taste

COCONUT CAULI MASH

1 large head cauliflower, roughly chopped
1 cup water
2 lime leaves (or a squeeze of lime juice)
Rest of the can of coconut cream
2 cardamom pods or ¼ tsp ground cardamom
Salt to taste

For the curry, sauté the brinjal, onion and peppers in coconut oil in a frying pan on medium to high heat, until soft. Add the chicken, garlic and ginger and cook for 5–7 minutes, stirring regularly. Add 1 cup of the coconut cream, followed by the peas and curry powder and allow to simmer, infuse and reduce a bit. Remove from heat and season to taste.

For the mash, steam the cauliflower in the water until cooked but not mushy. Drain the excess water and add the lime leaves, coconut cream and cardamom to the cauli chunks. Simmer gently and infuse for 3–4 minutes on low to medium heat. Remove cardamom and lime leaves and discard. Cook for 2–3 minutes while mashing and stirring as you go. Add salt. I prefer a very smooth cauli mash and always use a stick blender to purée the cauliflower after I remove the saucepan from the heat.

Serve a generous portion of curry on a serving of the coconut-infused cauli mash.

Yields 4 portions

Tomkin soup

CRAZY OR LAZY DAY QUICK TOMATO, PUMPKIN AND BACON SOUP OR, AS I LIKE TO CALL IT, TOMKIN SOUP.

RECIPE	PORTIONS	TOTAL CARBS	FIBRE	NET CARBS	FAT	PROTEIN	KJ
Tomkin soup	1	13.3 g	3.7 g	9.6 g	30.8 g	27 g	1 752

400 g pumpkin pieces
2–3 cups water or chicken stock
2 x 410 g cans whole peeled tomatoes or equal amount of passata sauce
1–2 Tbsp fresh parsley and thyme (small bunch fresh or use dried)
2 x 200 g packets diced bacon (cooked, but not too crispy)
1 cup fresh cream or coconut cream
Salt and black pepper to taste
1 Tbsp xylitol

In a large saucepan on medium-high heat, boil the pumpkin pieces in the water until soft. Drain the pumpkin and reserve the cooking liquid. Allow the pumpkin to cool slightly.

In a blender or food processor, blitz the canned tomatoes and the herbs and pour the mixture into a heavy-bottomed saucepan.

Blend the pumpkin and cooking liquid and add it to the tomato-herb mixture in the saucepan. Add the remaining ingredients and simmer for 5–10 minutes on medium heat.

Enjoy with grated Parmesan cheese or serve with a slice of low-carb bread or some fried halloumi strips to add some healthy fats.

Yields 4–6 generous portions

Hungarian cheesy beef and cabbage bake

RECIPE	PORTIONS	TOTAL CARBS	FIBRE	NET CARBS	FAT	PROTEIN	KJ
Hungarian bake	1	7.3 g	2.6 g	4.7 g	27 g	46 g	1 868

700 g beef mince
¼ cup butter
¼ tsp chilli flakes (optional)
½ tsp paprika
1 tsp crushed garlic
Salt and black pepper to taste
½ head cabbage, roughly chopped
3 spring onions, sliced
1 x 400 g can cherry tomatoes in juice (keep the can)
Big handful chopped fresh parsley
1 Tbsp xylitol
2 cups grated Cheddar cheese

In a large heavy-bottomed saucepan on medium to high heat, brown the beef mince in the butter. Add all the spices, garlic, salt and pepper. As soon as the meat starts to brown, add the cabbage and spring onions and sauté. As soon as the cabbage starts to turn translucent, add the tomatoes, parsley, a canful of water and xylitol. Turn the heat down to medium and allow the beef and cabbage to gently simmer while the liquid reduces.

When the sauce is thick and binds all the ingredients, top the dish with cheese, reduce heat to its lowest setting and cover with the lid in order to melt the cheese.

Serve as soon as the cheese has melted.

Yields 6 generous portions

SUMMER SOUP SIPPERS

THIS IS A WONDERFUL, REFRESHING WAY TO UP THE NUTRIENTS AND FIBRE, CLEANSE THE BODY, BOOST THE IMMUNE SYSTEM, ADD HEALTHY FATS AND AVOID THE OVEN. THESE SIPPERS MAKE FANCY STARTERS AND ARE WONDERFUL PALATE CLEANSERS TOO.

The 'soleado' summer sipper

SOLEADO MEANS 'SUNSHINE' IN SPANISH. THIS IS A BEAUTIFUL SIPPER WITH A LIGHT ORANGE HUE.

RECIPE	PORTIONS	TOTAL CARBS	FIBRE	NET CARBS	FAT	PROTEIN	KJ
'Soleado'	1 starter	8.2 g	3.3 g	4.9 g	25.9 g	2.5 g	1 032

¾ x 400 ml can coconut milk
½ cup frozen gooseberries
300–350 ml liquid vegetable stock concentrate
½ tsp ground cardamom
Thumb-size piece fresh ginger, grated
4 ice cubes

GARNISH
Avocado oil, toasted coconut flakes with a pinch cardamom

Place all the ingredients, except the garnish, into a blender and blend for 30 seconds. Garnish with a drizzle of avo oil, toasted coconut flakes and a pinch of cardamom. Serve immediately.

Yields 4 small starter sipper portions

DID YOU KNOW?
Cape gooseberries have more antioxidants than goji berries, broccoli or pomegranates. They also contain twice the vitamin C of lemons and are an excellent source of pectin. They are great for gut health, are anti-inflammatory and contain crucial minerals. The best news is that they are low carb too! Per 100 g serving you will count 5.7 g net carbs.

The 'affresco' summer sipper

AFFRESCO MEANS 'FRESH' IN ITALIAN.

RECIPE	PORTIONS	TOTAL CARBS	FIBRE	NET CARBS	FAT	PROTEIN	KJ
'Affresco'	1 starter	6.7 g	2 g	4.7 g	11.2 g	2.6 g	512
'Affresco'	1 full	13.5 g	4 g	9.5 g	22.4 g	5.2 g	1 020

4 fresh asparagus spears
2 medium baby marrows
10 cm piece cucumber, skin on
1 cup chopped spinach
100 ml liquid vegetable stock concentrate
¼ cup double-cream plain yoghurt
¼ cup fresh cream or coconut cream
¼ tsp crushed garlic
1 Tbsp fresh thyme leaves
4–6 ice cubes
½ cup cold water

GARNISH
2 Tbsp avocado oil, 100 g diced bacon (fried until crispy), sprigs fresh herbs, black pepper

Place all the ingredients, except the garnish, into a blender and blend for 30 seconds. Garnish with a drizzle of avo oil, bacon bits, a grind of black pepper and a herb sprig. Serve immediately.

Yields 4 small starter sipper portions or 2 full portions

The 'savoury lassie' summer sipper

RECIPE	PORTIONS	TOTAL CARBS	FIBRE	NET CARBS	FAT	PROTEIN	KJ
'Savoury lassie'	1 starter	8.8 g	2.7 g	6.1 g	31 g	2.8 g	1 224

1 x 400 ml can coconut milk
¼ tsp turmeric
½ tsp dried lemon grass or lime zest
Quick grind of black pepper
Pinch chilli flakes
1 cup fresh coriander leaves
Juice of 1 lime
½ medium cucumber, skin on
4 ice cubes

GARNISH
Avocado oil, black pepper and coriander leaves

Place all the ingredients, except the garnish, into a blender and blend for 30 seconds. Garnish with a drizzle of avo oil, a grind of black pepper and coriander leaves. Serve immediately.

Yields 4 small starter sipper portions

Platters and snacks

THIS CHAPTER INCLUDES A FEW FUN, THEMED PLATTER OPTIONS. MIX AND MATCH TO YOUR HEART'S CONTENT AND KEEP IN MIND THAT ALL PLATTERS CAN BE ACCOMPANIED BY YOUR CHOICE OF CHEESE AND VEGGIE STICKS OR LOW CARB FRUIT.

SUMMER HOLIDAY PLATTER

Hake nuggets in lettuce boats

RECIPE	PORTIONS	TOTAL CARBS	FIBRE	NET CARBS	FAT	PROTEIN	KJ
Hake nuggets	1 nugget	1.7 g	0.5 g	1.2 g	9.3 g	5.4 g	432

HAKE NUGGETS

3–4 eggs

6–8 Tbsp coconut flour

1–2 tsp fish seasoning spices

Salt and white pepper to taste

300 g hake fillets, cubed into 4 x 5 cm nuggets

½ cup coconut oil for frying fish

3 heads cos lettuce

Carb Smart™ mayo for drizzling

1 Tbsp toasted sesame seeds (optional)

SAUCE

3 Tbsp soy sauce

1 Tbsp xylitol

Juice and zest of 1 lemon

1 Tbsp grated fresh ginger or 1 tsp ground ginger

1 tsp crushed garlic

1 Tbsp apple cider vinegar

½ tsp chilli flakes

2–3 spring onions, finely sliced

Salt and pepper to taste

First prepare the fish. Whisk the eggs in a mixing bowl. In a deep dish plate, mix the coconut flour, fish seasoning and salt and pepper. Working in batches, dip the pieces of fish into the egg, then the flour and then then egg again.

In a heavy-bottomed pan on medium heat, heat the coconut oil and then add the nuggets in manageable batches. Fry for 2–3 minutes on each side or until golden brown all over. Set aside.

In a separate bowl, mix all the sauce ingredients together.

Return the nuggets to the pan, and add the sauce. Allow the sauce to simmer, thicken and infuse into the nuggets.

Let the nuggets cool a bit and then arrange into single lettuce leaf cups. Garnish with a drizzle of mayo and a sprinkling of toasted sesame seeds.

Yields 16–20 nuggets

Halloumi 'crackers' with sun-dried tomatoes and stuffed olives

RECIPE	PORTIONS	TOTAL CARBS	FIBRE	NET CARBS	FAT	PROTEIN	KJ
Option 1	1 'cracker'	2.1 g	1 g	1.1 g	11.6 g	5 g	419
Option 2	1 'cracker'	2.5 g	1 g	1.5 g	10 g	4.8 g	464

1 block halloumi cheese
2–3 Tbsp coconut oil

OPTION 1
1 tub storebought guacamole (preservative-free)
Stuffed olives (stuffed with nuts, lemon, garlic or feta)

OPTION 2
Sun-dried tomato pesto
1 tub storebought guacamole (preservative-free)
Sliced spring onions

Cut the block of cheese into 1 cm-thick strips and halve each strip into a bite-size cracker rectangle.

In a frying pan on medium to high heat, allow the coconut oil to melt and heat. Arrange pieces of the halloumi in the frying pan, leaving enough room to get a spatula in there to turn them over. Fry the cheese for 2–3 minutes per side until golden brown. (To serve as a cracker base, you want to have an extra crispy outside layer of halloumi.)

Arrange on a serving platter and add your chosen topping. Serve fairly hot.

Yields about 20 bite-size pieces

Cucumber 'crackers' with trout, crème fraîche and capers

RECIPE	PORTIONS	TOTAL CARBS	FIBRE	NET CARBS	FAT	PROTEIN	KJ
Cucumber crackers	1 'cracker'	1.5 g	>1 g	1.5 g	4.1 g	2.5 g	208

1 x 250 g tub crème fraîche
1 Tbsp each chopped fresh dill and chives
Black pepper to taste
12–15 x 1 cm-thick cucumber slices
100 g trout ribbons
2 capers per cucumber 'cracker'
Small lemon slices to garnish
Extra dill leaves or Tabasco sauce

In a mixing bowl, mix the slightly softened crème fraîche, herbs and pepper together and scoop into a piping bag. Make a pretty swirl on top of each cucumber 'cracker'.

Use the same number of trout ribbons as the cucumber crackers. Roll the trout ribbons into a swirl and plant firmly into the crème fraîche. Garnish with capers, a slice of lemon and some extra dill leaves or a dash of Tabasco sauce.

Yields 12–15 slices

Crunchy nori rolls with roasted seed butta dressing

RECIPE	PORTIONS	TOTAL CARBS	FIBRE	NET CARBS	FAT	PROTEIN	KJ
Crunchy nori rolls	1 roll	8.7 g	4.3 g	4.4 g	25.6 g	4.3 g	1 080

SPICED SOY SAUCE
6 Tbsp soy sauce
1 heaped tsp crushed garlic
1 heaped tsp grated fresh ginger
Pinch chilli flakes

ROASTED SEED BUTTA DRESSING (OPTIONAL)
½ quantity Roasted Seed Butta (p. 136)
¼ cup coconut cream mixed into it at the end

NORI ROLLS
4 sheets nori
8 lettuce leaves of choice (Italian or cos works well)
Wasabi paste (optional – for the brave ones only)
8 asparagus spears, halved
½ yellow pepper, thinly sliced
15 cm piece cucumber, deseeded and thinly sliced into matchsticks
1 medium baby marrow, thinly sliced into matchsticks
1 mini red cabbage, thinly sliced
8 radishes, thinly sliced
1 avocado, thinly sliced

Mix the spiced soy sauce ingredients together in a small bowl. Set aside.

Prepare the dressing as described in the recipe, adding the coconut cream just before serving to achieve a dipping consistency.

For the nori rolls, start by laying two lettuce leaves onto a sheet of nori. Drizzle with ½ Tbsp of the spiced soy sauce. Spread a thin layer of wasabi paste onto one asparagus spear half. Place four asparagus halves onto the lettuce, then add a quarter of each of the remaining vegetables. Tightly roll up the nori with the vegetables inside, and wet the edge with a little water to help it seal when you reach the end.

Repeat with the other sheets of nori and the rest of the vegetables. Slice the rolls in half. Serve immediately with the dressing.

Yields 8 portions

Garlic and herb stuffed mini buns

RECIPE	PORTIONS	TOTAL CARBS	FIBRE	NET CARBS	FAT	PROTEIN	KJ
Mini buns	1 bun	5.8 g	3.3 g	2.5 g	12.6 g	7.8 g	636

1 quantity Dough 1, with optional cheese (p. 14)

Coconut oil for frying

1 tsp crushed garlic

1 small onion, finely chopped

1 medium baby marrow, grated

1–2 Tbsp chopped fresh thyme, chives and oregano

Salt and pepper to taste

½ cup finely chopped meat, such as diced bacon, Pancetta or Italian ham (optional)

1 cup grated Cheddar or mozzarella cheese

1 egg, beaten

Preheat the oven to 180 °C. Line a baking sheet with baking paper.

Prepare the dough as described in the recipe.

While the dough rests, heat a little coconut oil in a pan on medium to high heat and sauté the garlic, onion, baby marrow, chopped herbs, salt, pepper and meat for 2–3 minutes. Allow the stuffing to cool slightly.

Divide the chilled dough ball into six equal portions. On a plastic wrap-covered chopping board, roll each portion into a 20 x 8 cm strip. (It will have naturally round edges – this is perfect.) Sprinkle the sautéed veggies, meat and cheese onto each piece. Starting at the bottom of each strip of dough, roll up to the top and cut each stuffed dough roll in half.

Place each roll, cut side facing down, onto the prepared baking sheet and press down slightly to stabilise. You can either make individual little buns, or pack them together into a stuffed bun wheel. Brush with the beaten egg and bake for 25–30 minutes.

Yields 12 stuffed mini buns

MEXICAN FIESTA PLATTER

Edible taco bowls with fillings

THIS IS A MESSY BUT FUN AFFAIR THAT KIDS AND TEENS WILL LOVE TOO. EAT YOUR MEAL, BOWL AND ALL (OR SERVE WITH A FORK AND PLATE FOR MORE SOPHISTICATED GUESTS).

RECIPE	PORTIONS	TOTAL CARBS	FIBRE	NET CARBS	FAT	PROTEIN	KJ
Edible taco bowls	1 taco	12.2 g	7.9 g	4.3 g	28 g	27.1 g	1 620

TACO BOWLS
1 quantity Dough 2, made with
1 cup sunflower seed flour + 1 cup
golden or brown flax meal (p. 17)
1 tsp salt
¼ tsp paprika
¼ tsp chilli flakes (optional)
½ tsp onion flakes (optional)
¼ tsp dried mixed herbs

FILLING
2–3 Tbsp coconut oil for frying
800 g–1 kg chicken or beef strips
½ tsp each ground cumin, ground
coriander, dried oregano, onion

flakes and chilli flakes (optional)
1 tsp each crushed garlic, paprika
and salt
Black pepper to taste

QUICK SALSA
2 medium ripe tomatoes,
deseeded and finely diced
½ medium red onion, chopped
1 small handful fresh coriander,
chopped
Pinch chilli flakes (optional)
1 tsp crushed garlic
Juice of 1 lime or ½ lemon
2–3 Tbsp extra virgin olive oil or

avocado oil
Salt and black pepper
1 tsp xylitol (optional)

TOPPINGS
4 cups shredded lettuce
2 avocados, cubed
1 cup grated Cheddar cheese
1 cup sour cream
Storebought guacamole (preservative-free) or make your own
Snipped chives for garnishing
Pitted black olives, roughly
chopped (optional)
Sliced fresh chillies

Preheat the oven to 180 °C. Turn a large 12-hole regular muffin pan upside down and butter the cups.

For the taco bowls, prepare the dough as described in the recipe, adding the extra spices to the dry ingredients before adding it to the butter-water mixture.

Line a large chopping board or flat surface with plastic wrap and use a rolling pin to roll out the chilled dough into a rectangle 3–4 mm thick. Using a 10 cm ramekin as a guide, cut out circles from the dough. Form another ball with the offcut pieces and repeat the process until you have used all of the dough. You need 12 circles for this recipe.

Use the bottom layer of plastic wrap as a support to lift and peel off the circles. Place the circles of dough over the upturned cups of the muffin pan – you will immediately see this takes the shape of a taco bowl. Bake for 10–15 minutes or until crisp and slightly browned. Gently remove each shell from the muffin pan and allow to cool standing upright.

For the filling, heat the coconut oil in a frying pan on medium to high heat, and then stir-fry the meat and all the spices until done.

For the salsa, mix all the ingredients together in a serving bowl. Place the filling, salsa and the topping ingredients in separate bowls for a help-yourself corner for your guests to assemble their own tacos.

Yields 12 tacos

FANCY FRENCH PÂTÉ AND BREAD PLATTER

Mini ciabatta loaves

RECIPE	PORTIONS	TOTAL CARBS	FIBRE	NET CARBS	FAT	PROTEIN	KJ
Mini ciabatta	1	13.3 g	9 g	4.3 g	27.3 g	9.1 g	1 240

1 quantity Dough 3 (p. 18)
1 egg, beaten
Salt to taste

Preheat the oven to 180 °C. Line a baking sheet with baking paper.

Prepare the dough as described in the recipe. Cover a large chopping board with a layer of plastic wrap. Shape and roll the chilled dough ball into a 1 cm-thick, 28 x 10 cm shape. Cut into four pieces of 7 x 10 cm each. Place on the prepared baking sheet and brush with beaten egg. Finish with a sprinkle of salt.

Bake for 25–30 minutes until crusty and golden brown on top.

Assemble with your favourite sandwich fillings and enjoy every blissful bite.

Yields 4 large ciabatta sandwiches

> **LEKKER TIP**
> Alternatively, create a quick platter made up of a few of your favourite cheeses, some veggies and Mini Savoury Doughnuts (p. 28). Serve with Cape Gooseberry and Rooibos Chutney (p. 137)

Mushroom and red wine pâté

RECIPE	PORTIONS	TOTAL CARBS	FIBRE	NET CARBS	FAT	PROTEIN	KJ
Mushroom pâté	1 bowl	15.8 g	3.1 g	12.7 g	44 g	76.5 g	3 384

2 Tbsp duck fat
1 medium red onion, chopped
1 tsp crushed garlic
1 Tbsp fresh mixed herbs of choice
1 cup chopped mushrooms of choice
Salt and pepper to taste
1 x 250 g tub chicken livers

TOPPING
1½ tsp gelatine powder
3 Tbsp water
½ cup red wine
1 Tbsp xylitol
½ tsp black pepper

In a frying pan on medium heat, melt the duck fat and sauté the onion, garlic, herbs, mushrooms and salt and pepper until soft and starting to brown a bit. Add the livers and cook for 6–8 minutes, making sure they are cooked through. Cool slightly.

Meanwhile, make the topping. In a small bowl, add the gelatine to the water and allow to bloom for a few minutes.

In a small saucepan, warm the red wine and then add the xylitol and black pepper. Stir in the gelatine until it dissolves.

In a blender (or using a stick blender), blend the pan juices along with the livers and veggies until a really smooth consistency is achieved. Pour into a 10–12 cm ramekin. Top with a layer of the red wine jelly and allow to set in the refrigerator for a few hours.

Yields 1 bowl of hearty pâté

Orange and rum chicken pâté

RECIPE	PORTIONS	TOTAL CARBS	FIBRE	NET CARBS	FAT	PROTEIN	KJ
Chicken pâté	1 bowl	20.7 g	5.8 g	14.9 g	98.4 g	63.4 g	4 932

2 Tbsp duck fat
1 medium red onion, chopped
1 Tbsp fresh mixed herbs of choice
1 cup chopped brinjals
1 tsp mixed spice
Salt and pepper to taste
1 x 250 g tub chicken livers
1 tsp crushed garlic

TOPPING
4 Tbsp duck fat
1 Tbsp xylitol
Zest of ½ orange
3 Tbsp orange juice
1 capful spiced rum
Pinch mixed spice

In a frying pan on medium heat, melt the duck fat and sauté the onion, herbs, brinjals, mixed spice and salt and pepper until soft and starting to brown a bit. Add the chicken livers and cook for 6–8 minutes, making sure they are cooked through before removing from the heat. Cool slightly.

Meanwhile, make the topping. Warm the duck fat in a small saucepan and add the xylitol, orange zest and juice and the rum. Allow to simmer and reduce for a minute or two.

In a blender (or using a stick blender), blend the pan juices along with the livers and veggies until a really smooth consistency is achieved.

Pour into a 10–12 cm ramekin. Top with a layer of the orange rum fat to seal, and sprinkle with a pinch of mixed spice. Allow to set in the refrigerator for a few hours.

Yields 1 bowl of hearty pâté

Rosemary and black pepper crackers

THESE CRACKERS ARE REALLY, REALLY CRISPY AND DELICIOUS. THE ADDED BONUS OF GELATINE GIVES THEM A SUPER FOOD BOOST.

RECIPE	PORTIONS	TOTAL CARBS	FIBRE	NET CARBS	FAT	PROTEIN	KJ
Rosemary crackers	1 round cracker	1.3 g	0.8 g	0.5 g	2 g	1.4 g	188

2 cups sunflower seed flour (or
1 cup sunflower seed flour + 1 cup
nut flour of choice)
1 tsp salt
1 Tbsp chopped fresh rosemary
1 Tbsp freshly ground black pepper
½ tsp bicarbonate of soda
125 g butter, melted
¼ cup milk, warmed slightly
2 Tbsp water
1 Tbsp gelatine powder
1 egg, beaten
1 cup grated Cheddar cheese (or
2–3 Tbsp grated Parmesan cheese)
2–3 Tbsp sesame seeds for rolling
or sprinkling (optional)

Preheat the oven to 180 °C.

Place the flour, salt, herbs, pepper and bicarbonate of soda in a mixing bowl.

In a small saucepan on medium heat, warm the butter and milk together, but don't let it boil.

In a small bowl, add the water to the gelatine and allow to bloom for a few minutes.

Remove the milk mixture from the heat and add the gelatine. Stir with a whisk until well combined and completely dissolved. Add the gelatine mixture to the dry ingredients and start to mix. Adding the beaten egg and cheese to the mix. Continue mixing by hand until the dough comes together to form a ball.

Place a sheet of plastic wrap on a cutting board and shape the buttery, sticky dough, using the sides of the plastic wrap to assist. The dough can be shaped into a log about 30 cm long, which can be dipped in sesame seeds, wrapped in plastic wrap, chilled in the freezer for 5–8 minutes and then cut into thin slices (yields 36 round crackers). Alternatively, roll out the dough sausage on a baking paper-lined 23 x 33 cm pan, and pre-cut into squares (yields 88 bite-size crackers). Wrap and allow the dough to set and chill in the freezer for a few minutes.

Bake for about 25 minutes until the cheese seeps through to the top of the crackers and appears melted, bubbly and brown. The crackers will harden upon cooling. Gently break into squares while still fairly warm to the touch.

Yields 48 crackers

MAFIA PLATTER

FOR WHEN YOU NEED TO 'KILL'... I MEAN, FILL THE MASSES.

Garlic, cheese, herb and olive focaccia

RECIPE	PORTIONS	TOTAL CARBS	FIBRE	NET CARBS	FAT	PROTEIN	KJ
Focaccia	1	8.4 g	5.2 g	3.2 g	15.4 g	8.2 g	768

1 quantity Dough 3 (p. 18)
1 egg, beaten
Salt to taste
1 Tbsp crushed garlic
1 handful fresh rosemary or other herbs of choice
8–10 black olives, pitted and halved
1 cup grated white Cheddar cheese or 3 Tbsp grated Parmesan cheese

Preheat the oven to 180 °C.

Prepare the dough as described in the recipe. On a sheet of baking paper and using a rolling pin, roll the chilled dough ball into a 1 cm-thick round base. Brush with the beaten egg and grind over some salt. Gently poke a few indents into the dough and sprinkle with the garlic, herbs, olives and cheese.

Bake for 25–30 minutes or until crusty at the bottom and golden brown on top.

Yields 1 focaccia cut into 8 medium portions

LEKKER TIPS

- For a more intense flavour, add 1 Tbsp finely chopped herbs to the dry ingredients before adding them to the butter-water mixture when making the dough.
- Try different toppings, such as thinly sliced onions, peppers, spring onions or mushrooms, and be adventurous with your herb selection.

Meatballs

RECIPE	PORTIONS	TOTAL CARBS	FIBRE	NET CARBS	FAT	PROTEIN	KJ
Meatballs	1 meatball	0.3 g	0 g	0.3 g	5.2 g	10.6 g	364

500 g beef mince
1 Tbsp BBQ spice (sugar-free)
Pinch smoked chilli flakes
(optional)
1 tsp salt
¼ tsp crushed garlic
1 egg
1 Tbsp chopped fresh parsley
Grind black pepper
3–4 Tbsp coconut oil for frying

Mix all the ingredients, except the oil, and roll into ping pong-size balls. In a frying pan on medium heat, fry the meatballs in the coconut oil for 8–10 minutes, turning regularly until browned and cooked through.

Yields 12–15 meatballs

> LEKKER TIP
>
> Double this recipe if your mob guest list is longer than the number of meatballs.

Green diva dip

THIS DIP IS A WONDERFUL WAY TO INCLUDE FIBRE, GUT-HEALTHY GELATINE AND NUTRIENTS – AND IT'S DELICIOUS TOO! THE MIXTURE CAN ALSO BE LEFT TO SET IN A PRETTY MOULD OVERNIGHT.

RECIPE	PORTIONS	TOTAL CARBS	FIBRE	NET CARBS	FAT	PROTEIN	KJ
Green diva dip	1 cup	15.8 g	5.4 g	10.4 g	43.6 g	12 g	1 916

3 Tbsp water
1 Tbsp gelatine powder
¼ cup melted butter
Handful fresh sage leaves
1 Tbsp chopped fresh herbs of choice
½ cup coconut milk
3 broccoli florets
3–4 asparagus spears
1 cup spinach
Juice and zest of 1 lime
50 g feta cheese
¼ tsp crushed garlic
Thumb-size piece fresh ginger, grated
2 Tbsp amasi
Salt and black pepper to taste

In a small mixing bowl, add the water to the gelatine powder and allow to bloom.

Warm the butter, sage, herbs and coconut milk together for 2–3 minutes. Add the gelatine and stir until it dissolves. Remove from the heat.

Pour the warm butter mixture and all the remaining ingredients into a blender and blend until it forms a purée.

Pour into a pretty bowl and use as a veggie dip or pour into a mould and refrigerate for a few hours.

Yields 2 cups

> LEKKER TIP
>
> This dip makes a lovely salad dressing too.

Caprese mould

RECIPE	PORTIONS	TOTAL CARBS	FIBRE	NET CARBS	FAT	PROTEIN	KJ
Caprese mould	Entire batch	11.5 g	2.5 g	9 g	44 g	17.3 g	1 992

3 Tbsp water
1 Tbsp gelatine powder
1 cup cherry tomatoes
5–6 fresh basil leaves
Salt and black pepper
¼ tsp crushed garlic
½ tsp chilli flakes
½ cup creamed cottage cheese

In a small bowl, add the water to the gelatine powder and allow to bloom. Blend the tomatoes, basil, seasoning, garlic and chilli flakes in a blender, then transfer the mixture to a small saucepan and heat on medium heat for 2–3 minutes. Stir the gelatine into the warm tomato juice until it dissolves. Remove from heat. Place the tomato mixture and cottage cheese into the blender and blend until well combined. Pour into a bowl and use as a veggie dip or pour into a mould and refrigerate for a few hours. Serve with veggie sticks and crackers.

Yields 2 giant cupcake-size moulds

Bacon crackers

RECIPE	PORTIONS	TOTAL CARBS	FIBRE	NET CARBS	FAT	PROTEIN	KJ
Bacon crackers	1 cracker	0.5 g	0 g	0.5 g	2.6 g	1.6 g	128

1 x 200 g packet streaky bacon
2 cups sunflower seed flour (or
1 cup sunflower seed flour + 1 cup
nut flour of choice)
½ tsp salt
1 Tbsp chopped fresh rosemary
1 Tbsp freshly ground black pepper
¾ tsp paprika
½ tsp bicarbonate of soda
2 Tbsp water
1 Tbsp gelatine powder
¼ cup melted butter
¼ cup milk, warmed slightly
1 egg, beaten
1 cup grated Cheddar cheese (or
2–3 Tbsp grated Parmesan cheese)
2–3 Tbsp sesame seeds for rolling
or sprinkling (optional)

Preheat the oven to 180 °C.

In a frying pan on medium to high heat, fry the bacon until crispy, making sure lots of the fat renders into the pan. Cool slightly. Scoop the bacon and fat into a blender. Purée as finely as possible.

Place the flour, salt, herbs, pepper, paprika and bicarb in a bowl. In another bowl, add the water to the gelatine and allow to bloom for a few minutes. Warm the butter and milk together but don't let it boil. Remove the milk from the heat and stir in the gelatine until it dissolves. Add the gelatine milk mixture as well as the puréed bacon mixture to the dry ingredients and start to mix. Add the beaten egg and cheese. Continue mixing until the dough comes together to form a ball. Wrap and allow the dough to chill in the freezer for a few minutes.

Place a sheet of baking paper on a cutting board and roll the dough into a rectangle to fit a 26 x 38 cm baking sheet. Slide onto the baking sheet and cut guidelines for your preferred size of cracker. Give one last generous grind of salt. Bake for about 25 minutes until the cheese seeps through to the top of the crackers and appears melted and bubbly brown. Cool and then cut or break into crackers.

Yields up to 88 crackers

Picnic
foods

Old-fashioned sausage rolls

RECIPE	PORTIONS	TOTAL CARBS	FIBRE	NET CARBS	FAT	PROTEIN	KJ
Sausage rolls	1 roll	15.1 g	8.8 g	6.3 g	37.6 g	61 g	2 252

1 quantity Dough 1, with optional cheese (p. 14)
1 egg, beaten
Salt to taste

MEAT FILLING
3 Tbsp butter or coconut oil
1 head cauliflower, roughly chopped
1 medium red onion, finely chopped
¼ tsp ground cloves
1–2 Tbsp BBQ spice (sugar-free)
Pepper to taste
1–1.2 kg beef mince
¼–½ cup of water
1 Tbsp apple cider vinegar (optional)

Prepare the dough as described in the recipe.

For the filling, heat the coconut oil in a heavy-bottomed saucepan on medium to medium-high heat and sauté the cauliflower, onion and spices for 3–4 minutes. Add the meat and brown it while the veggies continue to cook. Add the water, turn the heat down to medium and simmer with the lid half-on until the liquid evaporates. Allow the meat and veggies to cook completely until soft and dry. You do not want a filling with any excess liquid, as it will cause the dough to break apart. Start to mash the cauliflower into the meat using a potato masher. You need the cauliflower to act as a binder. Stir in the apple cider vinegar. Remove from heat and allow to cool.

Preheat the oven to 180 °C. Line a baking sheet with baking paper.

Line a large chopping board or flat surface with plastic wrap and roll out the chilled dough into a 45 x 25 cm rectangle. Cut the dough into three sheets measuring 15 x 25 cm. Fill each sheet with meat filling. Try to mould and compact the meat as much as possible before you fold the dough over. Tuck your hand under the plastic wrap and use it as a support to roll the dough over the meat filling. Roll the sausage over and place it seam side down onto the prepared baking sheet.

Repeat with the other two sheets of dough and remaining filling. Brush with the beaten egg and finish with a good grind of salt.

Bake for 25–30 minutes. Allow to cool, then cut each roll in half for a total of six medium sausage rolls. Alternatively, cut into smaller portions for cocktails or snacks.

Yields 6 sausage rolls

Cheeseburger picnic pies

RECIPE	PORTIONS	TOTAL CARBS	FIBRE	NET CARBS	FAT	PROTEIN	KJ
Cheeseburger pies	1 pie	13.9 g	8.5 g	5.4 g	42.6 g	44.1 g	2 396

2 quantities Dough 3 (p. 18), made
with 2 cups sunflower seed flour

PATTIES

1 kg beef mince
1 tsp dried mixed herbs
2 Tbsp BBQ spice (sugar free)
1 tsp garlic salt
Salt and pepper to taste
¼ cup coconut oil

TO SERVE

1 medium onion, sliced
10 slices tomato
2 cups grated Cheddar cheese
Pickle slices (lowest carb count)
1 egg, beaten
3–4 Tbsp toasted sesame seeds
(toasted in a dry pan until golden)

Prepare the dough as described in the recipe and allow to chill while you prepare the patties.

Preheat the oven to 180 °C. Line two baking sheets with baking paper.

In a mixing bowl, mix the mince, herbs and spices. Use your hands and firmly form eight compact meat patties between your palms. Sprinkle with a grind of salt and pepper on both sides.

In a large frying pan on medium to high heat, melt the coconut oil and fry the patties for 2 minutes on each side until lightly browned. The rest of the cooking will happen in the oven.

Let the patties rest on a chopping board while you sauté and caramelise the onion in the pan juices of the same pan.

Divide the chilled dough ball into two or three pieces to make rolling a bit easier. Roll out each piece of dough on a plastic wrap-covered cutting board. It needs to be 3–4 mm thick. Use a 12 cm ramekin to cut circles from the dough. Re-roll and repeat until you have 20 circles of dough.

Loosen the plastic wrap so that you can lift and peel off eight dough circles and place them onto the prepared baking sheets. Place the cooled patties in the centres of the dough circles. Top with onions, a slice of tomato, a handful of grated cheese and a pickle slice. Carefully peel and lift the other dough circles and place on top of the patties. Fold down the sides of the top circles and then use your hands to sculpt the bottom dough circles around the top ones. Press firmly and smooth out, ensuring the dough is sealed around the patties. Brush with the beaten egg and give a good sprinkle of sesame seeds. Bake for 25–30 minutes.

Allow to cool and then refrigerate until it's time for the picnic festivities to start (if you can wait that long, that is).

Yields 10 cheeseburger pies

LEKKER TIPS

• Once cooled, the baked burger pies can be frozen and kept in the freezer for up to six weeks.
• They are also perfect for lunchboxes and go really well with a light salad too.
• Use tomato pesto and mozzarella cheese instead of tomato slices and Cheddar for a bit of a gourmet touch.

Bull in a blanket

RECIPE	PORTIONS	TOTAL CARBS	FIBRE	NET CARBS	FAT	PROTEIN	KJ
Bull in a blanket	1	7.5 g	3.8 g	3.7 g	24.2 g	32.1 g	1 384

1 quantity Dough 3 (p. 18)
2 Tbsp coconut oil
10 x 10 cm lengths boerewors (or any good, cereal-free sausage)
1½ cups grated Cheddar cheese (optional)
1 egg, beaten
Salt to taste
Quick Home-made Marinara Dipping Sauce (optional, p. 113)

Prepare the dough as described in the recipe. Preheat the oven to 180 °C. Line a baking sheet with baking paper.

Heat the coconut oil in a frying pan and brown the boerewors or sausages for 2 minutes on each side until medium done. Set aside to cool.

Take the chilled dough ball and place on a plastic wrap-covered chopping board. Shape the dough into 30 cm-long strip. Cut into 10 equal-sized rectangles. Stretch each dough rectangle with your hands until it is roughly the same length as the sausages. Place a sausage in the centre of the dough and top with a bit of grated cheese, if using. Shape and press the dough around the sausage and cheese, and give a quick roll on the plastic wrap surface in order to even out the dough. Place the rolls onto the prepared baking sheet, brush with beaten egg and top with a grind of salt. Bake for 20–25 minutes or until the rolls are crusty and light golden brown.

Serve with the Marinara Dipping Sauce and a fibre-filled salad.

Yields 10 portions

LEKKER TIP
Double this batch and freeze for quick go-to snacks or kiddies' meals.

Easy sandwich sheets

FILL THEM, WRAP THEM, TIE THEM AND PACK THEM.

RECIPE	PORTIONS	TOTAL CARBS	FIBRE	NET CARBS	FAT	PROTEIN	KJ
Sandwich sheets	2 sheets	4.6 g	3.1 g	1.5 g	9.5 g	3.1 g	432

1 quantity Dough 3 (p. 18)
1 egg, beaten
Salt to taste
1 Tbsp sesame seeds (optional)

YOUR CHOICE OF SANDWICH FILLINGS, SUCH AS:
Roast beef, fried onions, herbs and cheese
Chicken or tuna mayo (using low-carb mayo), fresh
greens and veggies
Roast veggies, feta and bacon

Preheat the oven to 180 °C. Line two baking sheets (36 x 26 cm) with baking paper.

Prepare the dough as described in the recipe. Divide the chilled dough ball into two equal portions. Place each portion on its own baking sheet and roll out with a rolling pin until the dough covers the entire base.

Brush with the beaten egg and top with a few grinds of salt. Sprinkle sesame seeds on one sheet only.

Bake for 20–25 minutes or until the top is golden brown and the bottom is crusty and no longer sticks to the baking paper.

Flip one sheet over to face crust side up. Cut into 12 rectangles. Repeat with the second sheet – use the sheet with the sesame seeds as the top of your sandwich. Add your chosen filling.

Yields 12 sandwiches

LEKKER TIP

The sandwich rectangles can be stored in an airtight container for 3–4 days in the refrigerator. Alternatively, freeze in family-sized or lunchbox portions. Thaw and crisp up your easy sandwich bread by popping it into a toaster or just toast it because you love toast!

Basket o' bagels

RECIPE	PORTIONS	TOTAL CARBS	FIBRE	NET CARBS	FAT	PROTEIN	KJ
Savoury bagel	1 bagel	14.7 g	9.3 g	5.4 g	41.5 g	21 g	1 964
Sweet bagel	1 bagel	16 g	10.2 g	5.8 g	39.3 g	11.9 g	1 744

1 quantity Savoury Bagels (p. 14)
1 quantity Sweet Bagels made
from 1 quantity Dough 3 (p. 18)
Sunflower, sesame and poppy
seeds for topping (optional)

SAVOURY FILLING
2 Tbsp chopped fresh chives
½ tub or 125 g cream cheese
Salt and black pepper to taste
150–200 g smoked salmon

SWEET FILLING
1 tsp ground cinnamon
1–2 Tbsp powdered xylitol to taste
½ tub or 125 g cream cheese
OR
½ tub or 125 g cream cheese
½ cup fresh strawberry slices

Preheat the oven to 180 °C.

Prepare your choice of sweet and/or savoury dough balls as described in the recipes for Dough 1 (without optional cheese) and/or Dough 3 (for the sweeter version).

Divide each dough ball into four equal parts and roll each into a 20 cm sausage. Press the ends together to form a bagel shape. Brush with egg wash if you want a glossy bagel and top with your choice of seeds. Do the same for the sweet bagels, but omit the seeds. Bake for 20–25 minutes or until golden brown. Slice the bagels in half.

For the savoury filling, mix the chives into the cream cheese and add salt and black pepper. Spread the cream cheese mixture over the savoury bagels and top with smoked salmon.

For the sweet filling, mix the cinnamon and xylitol together. Spread the cream cheese over the sweet bagels and sprinkle with the cinnamon mixture. Alternatively, spread the bagels with cream cheese and top with the strawberry slices.

Yields 4 savoury and 4 sweet bagels

Spicy beef kebabs

RECIPE	PORTIONS	TOTAL CARBS	FIBRE	NET CARBS	FAT	PROTEIN	KJ
Spicy beef kebabs	1 kebab	4.9 g	1.2 g	3.7 g	10.5 g	27.6 g	868

700 g beef (use fatty, marbled, deboned sirloin or chuck), cut into 2 cm cubes

MARINADE
1 quantity Home-made Spice Blend (p. 57)
½ x 400 g can Indian flavour chopped tomatoes in juice
1 Tbsp xylitol
2 Tbsp olive or avocado oil
1 Tbsp apple cider vinegar
1 Tbsp grated fresh ginger
1 tsp crushed garlic
¼ large onion, cut into 2 cm cubes
¼ cup amasi or double-cream plain yoghurt

Mix all the marinade ingredients together in an airtight container and marinate the meat for at least 1 hour, but preferably 24 hours for the best results.

Thread the meat and cubes of onion onto skewers and braai over hot coals, fry in a frying pan or grill in the oven, turning often, until done and nicely charred.

Yields 8 kebabs

CHICKEN TIKKA KEBABS
Prepare the marinade as above, adding ¼ x 50 g sachet tomato paste. Use 700 g chicken breast fillets or deboned thighs, cut into 2 cm cubes.

LEKKER TIP
You can also use pork (roast or thick shoulder chops, cut into 2 cm cubes) for these kebabs.

Mini curry vetkoek

BE PATIENT WHEN FRYING THE VETKOEK BALLS – THEY NEED TO BAKE THROUGH TO THE CENTRE WITHOUT BURNING THE OUTER CRUST.

RECIPE	PORTIONS	TOTAL CARBS	FIBRE	NET CARBS	FAT	PROTEIN	KJ
Mini curry vetkoek	1 vetkoek	10 g	5.1 g	4.9 g	32 g	16.1 g	1 508

VETKOEK
1 quantity Dough 3 (p. 18)
1 cup coconut oil

CURRY IN A HURRY FILLING
2 Tbsp coconut oil for frying
1 medium onion, chopped
500 g beef mince
1 x 400 g can whole peeled tomatoes in juice
2 Tbsp mild and flavoursome curry powder
½ tsp crushed garlic
Salt and pepper to taste
1 Tbsp xylitol (optional)
1 cup diced pumpkin
1 cup sliced green beans
1 tsp turmeric
⅓ cup water

For the vetkoek, prepare the dough as described in the recipe. Roll the chilled dough ball into a thick rope about 36 cm in length. Cut into 12 pieces measuring 3 cm in length. Roll each piece into a ball.

In a heavy-bottomed pan, heat ¾ cup of the oil to medium heat. Fry a few dough balls at a time for 2–3 minutes per side, turning twice. Once the dough balls are golden brown all round, remove with a slotted spoon and allow to cool on a wire rack. Make sure the heat stays on medium and add a bit more oil before you put in a second batch of dough balls.

For the curry, heat the coconut oil in a heavy-bottomed saucepan on medium to high heat and sauté the onion for 2 minutes until soft. Add the mince and brown for 4–5 minutes. Once the meat starts to brown evenly, add the rest of the ingredients. Turn the heat down to medium and simmer gently for about 15 minutes. Stir occasionally and check the seasoning. You want the pumpkin to serve as a thickener or 'binder', so allow it to cook away into the curry. For the perfect vetkoek filling, reduce the curry to a consistency that is less saucy and more meaty and firm.

Allow the curry to cool and then scoop a heaped teaspoon or two into the mini vetkoek balls.

Yields 12 cocktail-size vetkoekies

Summer tarts

THIS RECIPE YIELDS 6–8 MEDIUM TARTLETS OR 1 LARGE SUMMER TART. I DO NOT GIVE EXACT QUANTITIES FOR THE FILLING OPTIONS, AS IT IS REALLY A MATTER OF PREFERENCE AND DEPENDS ON THE SIZE OF THE SHELL YOU ARE FILLING. THE RULE OF THUMB IS TO USE 2 CUPS OF YOUR MAIN VEGGIE/FRUIT, ¾–1 CUP MEAT, AND FILL IN THE REST TO TASTE.

RECIPE	PORTIONS	TOTAL CARBS	FIBRE	NET CARBS	FAT	PROTEIN	KJ
Option 1	6	9.0 g	2.7 g	6.3 g	37.4 g	18.6 g	1 732
Option 2	6	7.5 g	2.3 g	5.2 g	41.2 g	24.3 g	1 952
Option 3	6	8.5 g	2.9 g	5.6 g	37.4 g	21.2 g	1 776
Option 4	6	12.1 g	4.4 g	7.7 g	31.6 g	9.3 g	1 420
Option 5	6	9.5 g	2.8 g	6.7 g	30.4 g	7.5 g	1 324

1 quantity Dough 6 Savoury Pie Shell, made with 1 cup nut flour + 1 cup sunflower seed flour (p. 25)

CUSTARD
½ tub or 125 g crème fraîche
½ cup fresh cream
2 eggs
1 egg yolk
Pinch salt

FILLING OPTION 1
Cherry tomatoes , sliced mozzarella cheese, fresh oregano and basil, crushed garlic, salt and black pepper to taste

FILLING OPTION 2
Beef (strips, leftover roast beef or wet biltong), sliced Brie cheese, thinly sliced red onion rings or spring onions, pitted olives, fresh parsley and chives, crushed garlic, salt and black pepper to taste

FILLING OPTION 3
Baby marrow ribbons, asparagus spears , lamb sausage or strips from a chop, crumbled feta cheese, fresh rosemary and thyme, salt and black pepper to taste

FILLING OPTION 4
2 cups fresh or frozen gooseberries, fresh lemon thyme, thinly sliced red onion rings , sliced Camembert cheese, salt and black pepper to taste, 2 Tbsp xylitol

FILLING OPTION 5 (USE 1 QUANTITY DOUGH 6 SWEET PIE SHELL)
2 cups fresh or frozen mixed berries , 2 Tbsp xylitol, few drops vanilla extract (mixed into the custard)

Prepare the savoury or sweet batter as described in the recipe.

Preheat the oven to 180 °C. Grease 6–8 small flan pans or 1 large flan pan or line a 12-hole regular muffin or cupcake pan with paper cups.

Press a thin layer of dough into the prepared pan(s). Blind bake for 8 minutes.

In a mixing bowl, simply whisk all the custard ingredients together until well blended. Divide the custard between the pan(s), add your filling of choice and bake for 25–30 minutes for the small tarts or 45–50 minutes for a large tart. You will know it is ready when the custard starts to brown while firming up and puffing out. Allow to cool.

Top the savoury tart(s) with an extra grind of salt and pepper, fresh rocket or a drizzle of olive oil and a dash of balsamic vinegar.

Top the sweet tarts with a dusting of powdered xylitol and some edible flowers or herbs.

Yields 1 large tart or 6 tartlets

Mini quiche surprises

THIS IS THE ULTIMATE LEFTOVERS DISH. THERE REALLY ARE NO RULES AS FAR AS FILLINGS GO – HENCE THE SURPRISE ELEMENT. THE EGG BASE IS ENOUGH FOR EIGHT JUMBO MUFFIN CUPS. THESE ARE GREAT TO MAKE IN BULK.

RECIPE	PORTIONS	TOTAL CARBS	FIBRE	NET CARBS	FAT	PROTEIN	KJ
Mini quiche	1 quiche	2.2 g	0.5 g	1.7 g	13.5 g	13 g	740

EGG BASE
6 eggs
½ block or 125 g cream cheese
Pinch each salt and pepper

SNEAK IN SOME VEGGIES BY ADDING AND BLENDING ONE OF THE FOLLOWING TO YOUR BASE:
1 cup baby spinach
½ cup kale or Swiss chard
1 medium baby marrow
5 asparagus spears
4 broccoli florets

FILLING IDEAS
Chopped meat of choice, enough to fill one-third of the muffin cups
Chopped veggies of choice, enough to fill one-third of the muffin cups
Chopped fresh herbs of choice
Grated cheese for topping

Preheat the oven to 180 °C. Grease eight jumbo muffin cups.

For the egg base, place all the ingredients in a blender and blend for 10–15 seconds.

Arrange the meat and veggies in layers in the muffin cups. Pour in the egg base mixture and top with cheese and herbs. Bake for 20–25 minutes or until puffy and nicely browned.

Allow to cool and then freeze in portions or refrigerate in an air-tight container for snacks and lunchboxes.

Yields 8 mini quiches

Decadent pumpkin muffins

RECIPE	PORTIONS	TOTAL CARBS	FIBRE	NET CARBS	FAT	PROTEIN	KJ
Pumpkin muffins	1 muffin	6.5 g	2.3 g	4.2 g	19 g	4.4 g	832

¾ cup coconut flour
6 Tbsp sunflower seed flour or nut flour
2 Tbsp chia seeds (ground in a coffee grinder)
1 tsp bicarbonate of soda
½ tsp salt
1 tsp ground cinnamon
1 tsp mixed spice
3–4 Tbsp xylitol
½ cup melted butter
1 Tbsp apple cider vinegar
6 eggs
1 tsp vanilla extract
1 cup cooked, drained and mashed pumpkin
1 medium apple, grated
Chopped nuts for garnishing

CREAM CHEESE DOLLOP (OPTIONAL)
⅓ cup cream cheese, at room temperature
¼ cup unsalted butter, at room temperature
2–3 Tbsp powdered xylitol (made in a coffee grinder)
½ tsp vanilla extract

Preheat the oven to 180 °C. Grease a 12-hole regular muffin pan.

Mix the flours, chia seeds, bicarbonate of soda, salt, cinnamon, mixed spice and xylitol together. In a separate mixing bowl, mix the butter, vinegar, eggs, vanilla, pumpkin and grated apple together. Add the wet ingredients to the dry ingredients and stir gently for 1 minute, allowing the dry ingredients to absorb the wet ingredients.

Scoop the batter into the prepared muffin pan. Bake for 30 minutes. Allow to cool.

For the cream cheese dollop, use an electric mixer to beat the cream cheese, butter, xylitol and vanilla together. Drizzle over the muffins and top with nuts.

Alternatively, dust the cooled muffins with powdered xylitol and a sprinkling of cinnamon.

Yields 12 muffins

LEKKER TIP
Coconut cream makes for a lovely whipped cream topping. Refrigerate 1 x 400 ml can coconut cream for a few hours and whisk with an electric mixer until stiff peaks form.

Chocolate-dipped coconut

RECIPE	PORTIONS	TOTAL CARBS	FIBRE	NET CARBS	FAT	PROTEIN	KJ
Choc coconut	1 piece	1.2 g	0.4 g	0.8 g	1.6 g	0.2 g	80

½ coconut, flesh removed (opened by an expert or someone with anger issues)
Zest of 1 orange
½ x 100 g slab dark chocolate (85% or 90% cocoa solids)

Cut the coconut flesh into 1 cm strips and grate the orange zest. In a double-boiler or a glass mixing bowl suspended over a saucepan of simmering water, slowly melt the chocolate.

Line two baking sheets with baking paper. Dip the coconut strips halfway into the melted chocolate. Place on the baking paper to set and sprinkle with the orange zest. Keep refrigerated.

Yields 50+ pieces

Pizza-pull-apart bread

THIS IS A REAL CROWD-PLEASER AND A CONVERSATION PIECE IN ONE! SERVE HOT.

RECIPE	PORTIONS	TOTAL CARBS	FIBRE	NET CARBS	FAT	PROTEIN	KJ
Pizza bread	1	12.9 g	6.6 g	6.3 g	33.5 g	18.8 g	1 640

2 quantities Dough 3, made with
4 cups sunflower seed flour (p. 18)
1 x 125 g sachet tomato paste
1 Tbsp xylitol
2 tsp crushed garlic
Salt and black pepper to taste
1 x 250 g packet cooked and cubed
bacon, ham, pancetta, salami or
chorizo
2½–3 cups grated mozzarella
cheese
Generous handful chopped fresh
pizza herbs (oregano and basil)

BUTTER BAKING SAUCE
½ cup butter
½ tsp garlic salt
1 tsp dried Italian or mixed herbs
or 1 Tbsp chopped fresh herbs
Salt and black pepper

**QUICK HOME-MADE MARINARA
DIPPING SAUCE (OPTIONAL)**
1 x 400 g can peeled tomatoes in
juice – Italian herb flavour
1 Tbsp xylitol (optional)
Salt and black pepper to taste

Prepare a double batch of dough as described in the recipe.

Mix all the butter baking sauce ingredients together in a small saucepan and let them melt and infuse together on low heat. Allow to cool to room temperature.

Preheat the oven to 180 °C. Grease a Bundt cake pan.

In a separate bowl, mix the tomato paste, xylitol, garlic, and salt and pepper into a spreadable paste.

Take the chilled dough balls and place on a plastic wrap-covered chopping board. Roll out the dough into a single 35–40 cm-long strip. Cut into 14 equal-size pieces and roll each into a ball. Press each dough ball between the palms of your hands into a rustic circle a bit bigger than the size of your palm.

Spread about ¾ tsp of the pizza base sauce onto each round of dough. Now add the meat of your choice, a bit of grated cheese and lastly a few fresh chopped herbs. Gently fold and pinch the dough to look like a semi-crescent. Start packing each semi-crescent tightly into the prepared Bundt pan. Pour the cooled butter mixture evenly over the dough ring.

Bake for 45–50 minutes or until the dough ring is evenly browned. Tip the dough ring onto a cooling rack for 5 minutes, then transfer to a serving platter.

While you wait for the pizza ring to cool down, place all the marinara ingredients into a small saucepan and simmer for 5–7 minutes on medium heat until thickened and a deep red colour. Stir occasionally.

Place a pretty bowl into the centre hole of the pizza ring and fill with the marinara dipping sauce. Guests can now pull off a piece of pizza bread and dip it into the marinara sauce.

Yields 14 portions

Sweet pretzels

RECIPE	PORTIONS	TOTAL CARBS	FIBRE	NET CARBS	FAT	PROTEIN	KJ
Sweet pretzels	1 pretzel	9.2 g	6.2 g	3 g	18.2 g	6.1 g	832

1 quantity Dough 3, made with
1 cup nut flour + 1 cup sunflower
seed flour (p. 18)
1 egg, beaten
2 Tbsp xylitol mixed with 1 tsp
ground cinnamon

Prepare the dough as described in the recipe.

Preheat the oven to 180 °C. Line two baking sheets with baking paper. Lightly butter the baking paper.

Take the chilled dough ball and place on a chopping board covered with a layer of plastic wrap. Using both hands, roll the dough ball into an 18 cm-long sausage. Cut into six equal pieces. Now roll each piece into a 44 cm rope, position the rope on the greased baking sheet and twist into a pretzel shape. Brush with beaten egg and then sprinkle generously with the cinnamon-xylitol mix. Bake for 12–15 minutes or until the pretzels are firm and brown.

If desired, serve with Cream Cheese Dollop (p. 111).

Yields 6 pretzels

LEKKER TIP
Don't forget about the Mini Stuffed Buns (p. 84) or the Braai Scones (p. 22) – they make divine picnic companions.

Sides, salads
and condiments

SIDES

Roast cabbage medley

RECIPE	PORTIONS	TOTAL CARBS	FIBRE	NET CARBS	FAT	PROTEIN	KJ
Cabbage medley	1	12.2 g	5 g	7.2 g	20.6 g	2.5 g	928

½ head red cabbage
½ head small green cabbage
1 fennel bulb
150 g butter, melted
3 sprigs fresh thyme, leaves removed
2 Tbsp chopped fennel leaves
2 tsp crushed garlic
1 small red onion, chopped (optional)
Salt and black pepper

Preheat the oven to 200 °C. Line one or two baking sheets with baking paper.

Slice both cabbages and fennel bulb into 2 cm-thick discs. Mix the melted butter, herbs, garlic and onion in a separate bowl. Use a basting brush to liberally brush all the discs on both sides. Arrange the buttered discs on the prepared baking sheet(s). Grind over salt and pepper to taste. Bake for 10–12 minutes on each side or until the vegetables are nicely toasted or chargrilled around the edges. Add any leftover butter mixture during the process.

Yields 4–6 side portions

> **LEKKER TIP**
> Serve hot as a veggie side or cold as a salad. For a salad, cut the hard stem out of each cabbage disc, loosen the leaf layers and add crisply fried bacon or pancetta pieces. Drizzle with Sweet Mustard Vinaigrette (p. 135).

Veggie fritters

RECIPE	PORTIONS	TOTAL CARBS	FIBRE	NET CARBS	FAT	PROTEIN	KJ
Veggie fritters	1	5.6 g	2.6 g	3 g	21.7 g	6.4 g	924

4 large baby marrows
4 medium brinjals
6 cauliflower florets (with as much of the stem on as possible)
¼ cup grated Parmesan cheese
8 Tbsp coconut flour
½ tsp garlic powder
Salt and pepper to taste
6 eggs
¾ cup coconut oil for frying

Diagonally cut the baby marrows and brinjals into 5 mm-thick slices. Carefully cut the cauliflower florets into three intact slices. Mix the Parmesan, coconut flour, garlic powder and salt and pepper in a bowl and whisk the eggs in a separate bowl. Warm the coconut oil in a pan on medium heat. In small batches, dip the veggies into the egg, then into the flour mix. Dip into the egg again and then drop into the oil. Fry for 2 minutes on each side untill golden brown and crispy. Scoop out with a slotted spoon and repeat with the rest of the veggies.

Yields 8–10 snack platter portions

Baked leafy greens

RECIPE	PORTIONS	TOTAL CARBS	FIBRE	NET CARBS	FAT	PROTEIN	KJ
Baked leafy greens	1	7.4 g	1.7 g	5.7 g	16 g	8.7 g	804

180 g kale, stems removed and chopped
250 g chopped spinach
130 g crisp sweet lettuce, roughly chopped
2 Tbsp butter
½ tub or 125 g crème fraîche
Salt and black pepper
¼ cup fresh cream
1 egg
1 cup grated Cheddar cheese
¼ tsp nutmeg
½ small red onion, thinly sliced

Preheat the oven to 180 °C. Grease a medium ovenproof dish with a little butter.

In a heavy-bottomed saucepan on medium-high heat, sauté the leafy greens in the butter for 3–4 minutes. Add the crème fraîche, salt and pepper and saute for 3–4 minutes more before transferring the mixture to the ovenproof dish.

In a separate bowl, whisk the cream and egg together and stir in the grated Cheddar. Pour the cream mixture over the leafy greens. Sprinkle with nutmeg and loosely arrange the onion slices on top.

Bake for 15–20 minutes until set and lightly browned. Allow to cool slightly before cutting into block portions and serving.

Yields 4–6 side portions

Creamy turnip bake

RECIPE	PORTIONS	TOTAL CARBS	FIBRE	NET CARBS	FAT	PROTEIN	KJ
Turnip bake	1	8.5 g	1.8 g	6.7 g	12.4 g	5.9 g	704

4 medium to large turnips, peeled and thinly sliced
1 cup fresh cream (use coconut cream if dairy intolerant)
2 slightly heaped tsp turmeric
2 Tbsp butter
1 cup grated cheese (omit if dairy intolerant)
Salt and black pepper to taste

Preheat the oven to 180 °C. Grease an ovenproof dish.

Place a layer of turnip slices into the prepared ovenproof dish. Pour half the cream over the turnips. Sprinkle over 1 tsp turmeric and dot with half of the butter. Sprinkle with half the cheese and add seasoning. Repeat the layers, ending with a layer of cheese. Bake for 35–40 minutes.

Yields 4–6 side portions

Butter-fried cauliflower

RECIPE	PORTIONS	TOTAL CARBS	FIBRE	NET CARBS	FAT	PROTEIN	KJ
Fried cauliflower	1	10.3 g	3.7 g	6.6 g	11.9 g	2.6 g	596

1 Tbsp chopped fresh rosemary
¼ tsp crushed garlic
2–3 sun-dried tomatoes, finely chopped
¼ cup butter
1 head cauliflower, roughly chopped
1 medium red onion, chopped
Salt and black pepper to taste

Place the rosemary, garlic, sun-dried tomatoes and butter in a pan on medium heat and allow the butter to melt and the flavours to infuse before adding the chopped cauliflower and onion. Sauté slowly. Turn up the heat to medium-high after 4–5 minutes and chargrill and brown the cauliflower ever so slightly (don't stir too often). Add salt and pepper to taste.

Yields 4–6 side portions

LEKKER TIP

Bump this side up to a full meal by adding a pinch of ground cumin, 3 cups chopped kale, 8 cherry tomatoes, ¼ cup feta cheese and 4 grilled chicken thighs, deboned and chopped (skin on). Simply stir-fry these ingredients into the butter-fried cauliflower florets as soon as they start to char, giving the kale 1–2 minutes to wilt.

Spicy baked squash

RECIPE	PORTIONS	TOTAL CARBS	FIBRE	NET CARBS	FAT	PROTEIN	KJ
Baked squash	1	13.5 g	6.4 g	7.1 g	9.6 g	2.4 g	548

¼ small Hubbard squash
¼ pumpkin or butternut
1 medium brinjal, thinly sliced
¼ cup coconut oil for baking
1 box pilau rice spice blend (available from Woolies, or use a pinch each ground cardamom, ground cloves, ground cinnamon, black pepper and mustard seeds)
2 spring onions, thinly sliced
2 cloves garlic, thinly sliced
Handful fresh coriander leaves
1 tsp mild and flavoursome curry powder

Preheat the oven to 200 °C. Line a baking sheet with baking paper.

Slice the various squash and brinjal into 5 mm-thick rounds. Brush the coconut oil over the baking paper and place the veggies onto the oiled paper. Sprinkle half the pilau spices over the squash and brinjal and bake for 20 minutes or until they start to brown. Turn the veggies and sprinkle over the rest of the pilau spices, the spring onions, garlic, coriander and curry powder, and bake for another 8–10 minutes.

Enjoy hot or cold with some sour cream and Quick Salsa (p. 87), or simply as is.

Yields 6 portions

SALADS

Quick Asian salad

HIGH IN FIBRE AND HEALTHY FATS, AND EXTREMELY NUTRIENT DENSE. A COMPLETE MEAL ON ITS OWN. EITHER SERVE ALL THE COMPONENTS SEPARATELY AND LET EACH PERSON HELP THEMSELVES, OR COMBINE THEM ON A LARGE SALAD PLATTER.

RECIPE	PORTIONS	TOTAL CARBS	FIBRE	NET CARBS	FAT	PROTEIN	KJ
Quick Asian salad	1	13.8 g	5 g	8.8 g	20.7 g	30.9 g	1 376

¼ cup coconut oil
400–500 g steak of choice
Salt and black pepper to taste
1 x 250 g punnet mushrooms, sliced
10–12 fresh asparagus spears (optional, when in season)
6–8 long-stem broccoli, halved lengthways (regular is fine too)
Small handful carrots, julienned
2 medium baby marrows, julienned
1 x 250 g bag Asian lettuce or mix leafy lettuce of choice
1 x 200 g bag baby spinach
2 quantities Asian Crunch Salad Dressing (p. 136)
4 spring onions, thinly sliced diagonally

Heat some of the coconut oil and pan-fry or grill the steak to your personal preference. Season lightly with salt and pepper. Allow meat to rest before slicing into diagonal strips.

In a clean pan, add more coconut oil and stir-fry all the veggies, except for the lettuce, spinach and spring onions, until tender but still crunchy.

Arrange the lettuce and spinach leaves in a salad bowl or platter. Top with the veggie stir-fry, a few slices of beef, add the salad dressing for texture and flavour, and top with spring onions for crunch.

Yields 4–6 portions

Three-kinds-of-green salad

RECIPE	PORTIONS	TOTAL CARBS	FIBRE	NET CARBS	FAT	PROTEIN	KJ
Green salad	1	7.3 g	2.1 g	5.1 g	20.9 g	2.1 g	856

2 cups grated cucumber
2 cups French-cut green beans
(preferably fresh, but frozen will
do too)
1 Tbsp butter
2 medium baby marrows, grated
1 medium onion, chopped
Salt and black pepper to taste

BASIC VINAIGRETTE
8 Tbsp olive or avocado oil
2 Tbsp apple cider vinegar
2 Tbsp xylitol
¼ cup amasi
Salt and a grind of black pepper

Squeeze out some of the excess liquid from the cucumber. If you are using fresh green beans, lightly salt and sauté them in butter for 2–3 minutes. If frozen, boil the green beans in salted water for 2–3 minutes before transferring to iced water to halt the cooking process, or simply steam them for a few minutes. Drain and allow to cool completely.

Place all the grated and chopped veggies into a deep salad bowl.

For the dressing, add all the ingredients to a blender and blend for 30–40 seconds until thick and emulsified. Pour over the grated greens and chill well before serving.

Yields 4–6 side salad portions

Tikka calamari salad

THIS SALAD IS DELICIOUSLY SPICY – ENJOY A GENEROUS PORTION.

RECIPE	PORTIONS	TOTAL CARBS	FIBRE	NET CARBS	FAT	PROTEIN	KJ
Calamari salad	1	12.9 g	4.1 g	8.8 g	18.7 g	20.1 g	880

600 g calamari rings or strips (cut calamari steaks into strips while still frozen)

MARINADE
1 heaped Tbsp chicken tikka spices (I use the Woolies brand)
¼ cup amasi
Juice and zest of 1 small lemon
1 Tbsp xylitol
¼ cup avocado oil
¼ tsp crushed garlic
¼ tsp chilli flakes (optional)
1 Tbsp grated fresh ginger
Salt and black pepper to taste
Coconut oil for frying

SALAD
1 x 300 g bag butter lettuce leaves
12 cherry tomatoes, halved
1 avocado, cubed
1 small red onion, thinly sliced
⅓ cucumber, thinly sliced
12 black olives
1 x 100 g packet herbed feta balls or 1 wheel feta cheese, diced

Thaw the calamari rings if frozen. Mix all the marinade ingredients together, except for ½ Tbsp of the tikka mix. Add the calamari to the marinade, cover with plastic wrap and refrigerate for 20–30 minutes.

Meanwhile, assemble the salad ingredients.

Lift the calamari from the marinade and gently shake off the excess liquid. Reserve the leftover marinade. Heat the oil well in a pan on high heat, then add the calamari and the reserved ½ Tbsp tikka mix. Fry for 1–2 minutes or until it is no longer transparent. (If there is excess liquid in the pan, drain it quickly and resume cooking for a few seconds.) Place the calamari on a plate to cool slightly.

Leave the pan on high heat and add the leftover marinade. Allow to thicken and reduce for 2–3 minutes.

Add the calamari to the salad base and drizzle with the thickened marinade. Serve immediately.

Yields 2–3 main course portions or 4 lunch or starter portions

SALAD STACKS

WE EAT A LOT OF GREEN TABLE SALADS, THE KIND YOU TOSS TOGETHER IN MINUTES TO UP OUR NUTRIENT BASE AND FIBRE INTAKE, BUT THESE LITTLE STACKS BRING A BIT OF WHIMSY AND A TASTE EXPLOSION WITH EACH BITE. I LOVE THIS CONCEPT. EVEN THOUGH IT TAKES A BIT MORE TIME TO PREP OR ASSEMBLE, IT MAKES A DIVINE STARTER FOR A SPECIAL DINNER PARTY AND CAN EVEN BE TRANSPORTED IN THE SILICONE CUP AND TIPPED ONTO THE LETTUCE FOR A PRETTY PICNIC DISH. PREPARE TO FALL IN LOVE...

Italian salad stack

THIS IS THE RECIPE YOU SHOULD TURN TO WHEN A HOLIDAY IS LONG OVERDUE.

RECIPE	PORTIONS	TOTAL CARBS	FIBRE	NET CARBS	FAT	PROTEIN	KJ
Italian salad stack	1	16.9 g	5.9 g	11 g	21 g	24.5 g	1 364

MEAT

Coconut oil for frying and baking
2 chicken breast fillets, cubed
½ tsp crushed garlic
1 Tbsp chopped fresh rosemary and oregano or 1 tsp dried Italian herbs
3 Tbsp chopped sun-dried tomato
12 black olives, pitted and chopped
Juice of 1 small lemon
Salt and black pepper

VEGGIES

1 yellow pepper, sliced
4 medium baby marrows, sliced into ribbons with a veggie peeler
8 fresh asparagus spears, chopped (optional)
2 medium brinjals, sliced into 5 mm-thick rounds and sprinkled with salt
½ cup double-cream plain yoghurt
1–2 sprigs fresh mint, chopped
1 cup grated mozzarella cheese
1 x 100–150 g bag baby spinach and rocket leaf mix
Caper berries for garnishing (completely optional, but worth it)

In a pan on medium to high heat, add some coconut oil and stir-fry the chicken, garlic and herbs for 3–4 minutes. Add the sun-dried tomato, olives, lemon juice and salt and pepper to taste. Adjust to medium heat and simmer and infuse flavours for a minute or two. Remove from pan and allow to cool slightly.

In the chicken pan juices, sauté the yellow pepper, baby marrow ribbons and asparagus. Allow the veggies to caramelise slightly before removing them from the pan. Rinse the salt from the brinjal slices and pat dry. Add a little more oil to the pan and fry the brinjal rounds on medium heat, turning occasionally until soft and slightly golden.

In a small bowl, mix the yoghurt and mint together and add a pinch of salt.

Use four large silicone muffin cups and start layering the still-warm salad stack. Gently press the chicken into the silicone cups and layer some overlapping brinjal rounds over the chicken layer, followed by a layer of baby marrow ribbons, and then asparagus. Seal the deal with a helping of grated mozzarella that you gently press to compact the layers a bit. The warm veggies will melt the mozzarella slightly. Allow to cool and place in the refrigerator until you are ready to serve.

Arrange the salad greens on individual serving plates and then take the plunge and tip each mould onto the bed of leafy greens. Top with a dollop of minted yoghurt and garnish with a grind of black pepper and caper berries.

Yields 4 portions

BLT salad stack

RECIPE	PORTIONS	TOTAL CARBS	FIBRE	NET CARBS	FAT	PROTEIN	KJ
BLT salad stack	1	8.3 g	2.6 g	5.7 g	43.5 g	25.6 g	2 092

Coconut oil for frying
1 x 200 g packet bacon bits
1 red or orange pepper, sliced
1 small red onion, sliced
¼ tsp crushed garlic (optional)
½ tub or 125 g crème fraîche or full-fat cottage cheese
1–2 Tbsp chopped fresh herbs of choice (chives and thyme work well)
8 cherry tomatoes, thinly sliced into rounds
10 cm piece cucumber, diced into 1 cm cubes
4 cups finely chopped lettuce
¼ cup grated Cheddar cheese
¼ cup olive oil
Salt and black pepper

In a frying pan with a bit of coconut oil, fry the bacon bits until crispy. Remove from the pan and divide into four equal portions. Set aside to cool.

In the bacon pan juices, sauté the red pepper and onion slices and add the crushed garlic if using. Allow the veggies to caramelise slightly before removing from heat.

In a small bowl, mix the crème fraîche and herbs together.

Use four large silicone muffin cups and start layering the salad stack. Gently press the bacon bits into the silicone cups and 'cement' it together with a generous tablespoonful of herbed crème fraîche. Now layer some overlapping tomato rounds and cucumber cubes onto the crème fraîche layer and follow with some caramelised peppers and onions. Gently press to compact the layers a bit and place in the refrigerator until you are ready to serve.

Arrange the lettuce on individual serving plates and sprinkle with some grated cheese. Tip each mould onto the bed of leafy greens. Drizzle with olive oil and season with salt and black pepper.

Yields 4 portions

Kipper salad stack

A GREAT RECIPE FOR A LOVELY BRUNCH.

RECIPE	PORTIONS	TOTAL CARBS	FIBRE	NET CARBS	FAT	PROTEIN	KJ
Kipper salad stack	1	9.7 g	4.7 g	5 g	31 g	22.2 g	1 560

1 x 200 g kipper fillet (boiled in a bag with butter, or get it from Woolies)
½ tub or 125 g crème fraîche or full-fat cottage cheese
1 Tbsp finely chopped fresh herbs of choice (dill, chives, parsley or coriander works well)
2 spring onions, chopped
10 cm piece cucumber, diced into 1 cm cubes
4 hard-boiled eggs, sliced
1 avocado, cubed
1 x 150–200 g packet baby rocket and spinach leaves
¼ cup olive oil
Juice and zest of 1 lime or medium lemon
A grind of black pepper

Follow the instructions on the packaging and boil the kipper fillet in its butter sauce. Allow to cool completely and then flake gently into four equal portions.

In a small bowl, mix the crème fraîche and herbs together.

Use four large silicone muffin cups and start layering the salad stack. Gently press the flaked kipper into the silicone cups, add a layer of spring onions and 'cement' it together with a generous table-spoonful of herbed crème fraîche. Now secure the cucumber cubes onto the crème fraîche layer and follow with some overlapping egg slices. Gently press to compact the layers a bit and top with the cubes of avo. Either place in the refrigerator until you are ready to serve or move on to the finish line.

Arrange the salad greens on individual serving plates and then take the plunge and tip each mould onto the bed of leafy greens. Drizzle with olive oil and add a squeeze of lime juice, some zest and a grind of black pepper.

Yields 4 portions

Summer salad with strawberry poppy vinaigrette

RECIPE	PORTIONS	TOTAL CARBS	FIBRE	NET CARBS	FAT	PROTEIN	KJ
Summer salad	1	14.8 g	6.7 g	8.1 g	29.5 g	6.4 g	1 332

2 cups baby spinach
3 cups shredded lettuce
1 avocado, cubed
½ cup frozen minted peas, thawed
1 small red onion, thinly sliced
¼ cup pecan nuts, roughly chopped
½ cup cubed feta cheese
½ cup sliced or whole fresh berries of choice
1 quantity Strawberry Poppy Vinaigrette (p. 135)

Assemble all the ingredients in jars for a pretty addition to a picnic or make in a large salad bowl.

Serve with strawberry poppy vinaigrette.

Yields 2 large or 4 side salads

LEKKER TIP
Bump this salad up to a full meal by adding biltong slices, bacon bits or cubes of smoked chicken.

Grilled chicken satay salad with roasted seed butta dressing

RECIPE	PORTIONS	TOTAL CARBS	FIBRE	NET CARBS	FAT	PROTEIN	KJ
Chicken satay salad	1	11.7 g	4.5 g	7.2 g	39 g	19.7 g	1 836

3 chicken breast fillets, skin on
1 quantity Roasted Seed Butta Dressing (p. 83)

MARINADE
1 tsp mild curry powder
½ tsp turmeric
¼ tsp chilli flakes (optional)
¼ cup coconut milk
Juice and zest of 1 lime
1 Tbsp xylitol
1 Tbsp soy sauce
3 Tbsp coconut oil for frying
Salt and black pepper to taste

SALAD
½ cup gooseberries
½ cup cherry tomatoes, halved
4-6 radishes, thinly sliced
1 cup thinly sliced red cabbage
3 cups thinly sliced green cabbage
3 spring onions, chopped
½ cup frozen peas, thawed

Set your oven to grill. Brush a baking sheet with coconut oil.

Cut the chicken fillets into 2 cm cubes. Place all the marinade ingredients in a zip-seal bag and add the cubes of chicken. Let it marinate in the refrigerator for 10–15 minutes. String the chicken cubes onto eight skewers and place on a wire rack. Allow the excess marinade to drip off. Line the baking sheet with the skewers and grill for 10–15 minutes, or until nicely charred (turn from time to time).

On a large serving platter, arrange all the salad ingredients, except the peas, in clusters. Place the chicken skewers on one side of the platter. Loosely scatter the peas over the entire platter.

Drizzle some of the Roasted Seed Butta Dressing over the skewers and salad and serve the rest separately.

Yields 4–6 portions

Quick Mexican salad tacos

FOR THOSE SUMMER EVENINGS WHEN YOU NEED TO TURN A HEAT WAVE INTO A MEXICAN WAVE.

RECIPE	PORTIONS	TOTAL CARBS	FIBRE	NET CARBS	FAT *	PROTEIN	KJ
Salad tacos	1	13.9 g	6 g	7.9 g	36.8 g	53.6 g	2 392

SALSA

1 small red onion, finely chopped

1 cup cherry tomatoes, quartered
or 1 large tomato, chopped

Handful fresh coriander leaves,
chopped (optional)

½ tsp crushed garlic

1 Tbsp olive oil

Juice of ½ lemon

Salt and pepper to taste

30-SECOND MEXICAN DRESSING

¼ cup double-cream plain yoghurt

1 Tbsp xylitol

½ tsp curry powder

¼ tsp chilli flakes (optional)

¼ tsp ground cumin

¼ tsp dried lemon grass

1 Tbsp chopped fresh oregano
or ½ tsp dried oregano

Squeeze of lemon juice

Salt and pepper to taste

TACOS

1 large head crisp sweet lettuce or
250 g cos lettuce

500 g leftover, shredded chicken,
roast beef, beef mince or tuna

1 Tbsp BBQ spice (sugar-free)
(optional)

½ tsp ground cumin

½ tsp crushed garlic

Salt and pepper to taste

1–2 cups grated white Cheddar
cheese

1 tub storebought guacamole
(preservative-free)

First, combine all the salsa ingredients in a small bowl, stir and chill until needed.

Next, place all the Mexican dressing ingredients in a blender and blend for 10–20 seconds. Pour into a serving jug.

To make the tacos, remove the lettuce leaves from the stem and rinse. These leaves form nice deep serving bowls, which is perfect for filling and holding.

Mix your choice of meat with the BBQ spice, cumin, garlic and salt and pepper.

Set out the lettuce leaves, meat, salsa, dressing, cheese and guacamole and allow guests to assemble their own lettuce tacos.

Yields 4–6 portions

LEKKER TIP

Turn this family fiesta into a very budget-friendly friends and family feast by adding chopped olives, sour cream and jalapeños for the brave ones. Cook a *mucho grande* (very big) beef roast in a slow-cooker for 7–8 hours with some water, onion, garlic, salt and pepper. Shred the cooked beef with two forks and set out with the rest of the components. All you need now is to send in the Mariachi band!

Retro cucumber and avo ring

COME ON YOU HIPSTERS... YOU KNOW YOU WANT TO!

RECIPE	PORTIONS	TOTAL CARBS	FIBRE	NET CARBS	FAT	PROTEIN	KJ
Cucumber avo ring	1	5.9 g	2.7 g	3.2 g	13.2 g	2.9 g	576

2 Tbsp + ½ cup water
1 Tbsp gelatine powder
¾ cup coconut cream
1 cup mashed avocado
Juice of ½ lemon
2 Tbsp cream cheese
½ tsp crushed garlic
½ cucumber, grated and drained
3 Tbsp chopped fresh chives
2 Tbsp chopped fresh dill
Salt and pepper to taste

Add the 2 Tbsp water to the gelatine powder and allow to bloom for a few minutes. In a medium-sized saucepan on high heat, bring the ½ cup of water to a boil and add the bloomed gelatine. Stir until fully dissolved and then remove from heat. Add the coconut cream, stir and allow to cool for 2–3 minutes while you prepare the avo mixture.

In a blender, blend the avocado, lemon juice, cream cheese and garlic together until combined.

In a separate mixing bowl, combine the gelatine mixture, avo mixture, cucumber, herbs, and salt and pepper, and mix to a smooth, well blended consistency. Pour into a ring mould and refrigerate for 1–2 hours until set.

Unmould onto a serving platter and fill the centre with a pretty salad. I like to use spicy olives, rocket, mange tout, cocktail tomatoes and sliced Emmental cheese.

Yields 6–8 portions

CONDIMENTS

Avonnaise salad dressing

RECIPE	PORTIONS	TOTAL CARBS	FIBRE	NET CARBS	FAT	PROTEIN	KJ
Avonnaise	Entire batch	21.1 g	13.5 g	7.6 g	81.8 g	6.5 g	3 232

1 avocado, peeled and halved
3 Tbsp light olive oil, extra virgin olive oil or avocado oil
1 Tbsp apple cider vinegar
1 Tbsp xylitol
3 Tbsp amasi
½ tsp crushed garlic
Salt and freshly ground black pepper to taste

Place all the ingredients into a blender and blend for 30 seconds. Use immediately.

Yields enough for one family-size salad

60-second tzatziki salad dressing

THIS IS A LOVELY DRESSING, ESPECIALLY FOR THOSE TIMES OF THE YEAR WHEN AVOCADOS ARE SIMPLY TOO PRICY.

RECIPE	PORTIONS	TOTAL CARBS	FIBRE	NET CARBS	FAT	PROTEIN	KJ
Tzatziki dressing	Entire batch	11 g	2.6 g	8.4 g	39.2 g	2.8 g	1 536

10 cm piece cucumber, skin on
2 spring onions
2–3 Tbsp double-cream plain yoghurt or coconut cream
2 Tbsp avocado or olive oil
Juice of ¼ lemon
1 Tbsp xylitol
¼ tsp crushed garlic
Salt and freshly ground black pepper to taste

Place all the ingredients into a blender and blend for 30 seconds. Store in the refrigerator for 2–3 days.

Yields enough for 1–2 family-size salads

Sweet mustard vinaigrette

RECIPE	PORTIONS	TOTAL CARBS	FIBRE	NET CARBS	FAT	PROTEIN	KJ
Mustard vinaigrette	Entire batch	2.2 g	0.9 g	1.3 g	85 g	0.9 g	2 992

6 Tbsp olive oil or avocado oil
3 Tbsp apple cider vinegar
3 Tbsp water
1 Tbsp xylitol
¼ tsp salt
Pinch pepper
1 tsp fresh thyme leaves
1 tsp mustard powder

Put all the ingredients in a small bowl and whisk swiftly with a hand whisk in order to emulsify the oils. Alternatively, double the ingredients and blend until emulsified. Keeps in the refrigerator for 5–7 days.

Yields enough for 1–2 salads

Strawberry poppy vinaigrette

RECIPE	PORTIONS	TOTAL CARBS	FIBRE	NET CARBS	FAT	PROTEIN	KJ
Vinaigrette	Entire batch	5 g	1.4 g	3.6 g	44.1 g	1.1 g	1 616

3–4 fresh or frozen strawberries
3 Tbsp olive oil or avocado oil
1 Tbsp apple cider vinegar
Pinch salt
½ Tbsp xylitol
3 Tbsp water
½ Tbsp poppy seeds

Put all the ingredients in a blender and blend for 30–45 seconds. Keeps in the refrigerator for 5–7 days.

Yields ½ cup

Roasted seed butta

RECIPE	PORTIONS	TOTAL CARBS	FIBRE	NET CARBS	FAT	PROTEIN	KJ
Roated seed butta	Entire batch	19.8 g	7.9 g	11.9 g	59.8 g	18.8 g	2 604

¼ cup pumpkin seeds
1 cup sunflower seeds
¼ cup coconut flakes or desiccated coconut
1 Tbsp coconut oil for roasting
1 Tbsp xylitol
½ tsp ground cinnamon
¼ tsp ground cardamom
¼ tsp vanilla extract
½ tsp salt (or more to taste)
½ cup melted coconut oil or avocado oil

In a pan on medium heat, roast the seeds and coconut flakes for about 3 minutes in 1 Tbsp coconut oil until golden. Stir occasionally to ensure they roast evenly.

Add the xylitol, cinnamon, cardamom, vanilla and salt, and remove from heat. Add the oil and blend into a super-fine paste in your blender.

If you only have a stick blender, rather dry-roast the seeds and omit the tablespoon coconut oil. Place the spice-infused seed mix into a coffee grinder in batches to make a fine roasted flour. Add the oil to the seed flour and blend into a paste with the stick blender. Keeps in the refrigerator for 7–10 days.

Yields 1½ cups

Asian crunch salad dressing

RECIPE	PORTIONS	TOTAL CARBS	FIBRE	NET CARBS	FAT	PROTEIN	KJ
Asian dressing	1	2.2 g	0.6 g	1.6 g	7 g	1.6 g	300

3 Tbsp sunflower seeds
2 Tbsp sesame seeds
¼ tsp dried lemon grass
¼ tsp chilli flakes
¼ tsp ground ginger or ½ thumb-size piece fresh ginger, grated
Pinch ground cumin
1 Tbsp xylitol
¼ cup soy sauce
2 Tbsp avocado oil, olive oil or melted coconut oil
½ tsp crushed garlic or garlic powder
Juice and zest of 1 small lemon or regular lime
Black pepper to taste

Dry roast the seeds, lemon grass, chilli flakes, ground ginger (if using), cumin and xylitol in a pan on medium heat. The xylitol will melt into the seeds and, once cooled, will become sticky and form little crunchy clusters.

In a separate bowl, mix all the wet ingredients, including the garlic, fresh ginger (if using) and zest if you are using fresh ingredients.

Combine the seed clusters and sauce minutes before serving or sprinkle the seed clusters on your salad and drizzle the sauce over the top.

Use immediately so that you don't lose the crunch element. Alternatively, keep the seeds and vinaigrette separate in the refrigerator for up to seven days, and only combine just before using.

Yields enough dressing for 1 large salad

Cape gooseberry and rooibos chutney

THIS RECIPE IS MY ODE TO THE BOLAND AND SURROUNDS, THE PLACE WHERE I PLANTED MY HEART...

RECIPE	PORTIONS	TOTAL CARBS	FIBRE	NET CARBS	FAT	PROTEIN	KJ
Chutney	1 Tbsp	1.9 g	0.6 g	1.3 g	0.1 g	0.2 g	36

1 cup fresh or frozen gooseberries
1 medium red onion, sliced
1 heaped tsp curry powder
½ tsp turmeric
1 tsp crushed garlic
¼ cup xylitol
1½ Tbsp apple cider vinegar
1 cup rooibos tea concentrate
(made from ½ cup boiling water
and 4 rooibos tea bags)

Place the gooseberries, onion, spices, garlic and xylitol in a small saucepan on medium to high heat. Stir gently until the xylitol has dissolved and then add the vinegar. Bring to a boil and simmer for 3–5 minutes. Add the tea concentrate and simmer on medium heat for 8–10 minutes or until thick, glossy, slow-bursting bubbles appear.

Scoop into a sterilised jar and refrigerate. Use within 7–10 days. This chutney pairs perfectly with an array of cheeses and is delicious on Veggie Fritters (p. 117).

Yields 1 cup

For the
kids

Many of the recipes in this book are family friendly. Even the spicy dishes can be made child friendly by omitting some of the spices. Mostly, my family eats very simple, real food meals, and as far as snacks go frozen blueberries during a Wellington heat wave seemed to tick all the boxes for my one-year-old twins.

I put this chapter together to provide some age-appropriate, whole food snack and treat ideas. Although these are unprocessed, good-for-you kinds of snacks, they don't have to be on the daily menu. I have so often felt like the worst mom in the world when, during crazy times, we simply don't have baked goods in the house. On these days, snacks are simply carrots, celery, cucumbers, cheese and the occasional chunk of dark chocolate I forgot I had hidden in the freezer.

NB!
A friendly reminder for animal lovers with young children: NEVER give any food containing xylitol to dogs as it is highly toxic to them, even in tiny doses. Take care that little explorers don't share their treats with pets. Consider using erythritol natural sweetener instead of xylitol; it works in the same way but isn't harmful to animals. Although it is more difficult to come by, it can be purchased online or at Dis-Chem.

FIRST SNACKS: 8+ MONTHS

NO TWO BABIES ARE THE SAME. BELIEVE ME, I KNOW; I HAD TWO AT ONE GO AND THEY DID NOT HAVE THE SAME NIGGLES OVER THE SAME FOODS. YOU HAVE TO EXPLORE TOGETHER AND FIND THE HAPPY MIDDLE GROUND.
THIS NEXT RECIPE WAS EXACTLY THAT FOR OUR TWIN GIRLS. AT FIRST I ONLY MADE A SANDWICH SHEET THAT I WOULD CUT INTO BITE-SIZE CUBES. IT IS EGG AND NUT FREE AND CAN BE COMPLETELY DAIRY FREE IF YOU USE COCONUT OIL INSTEAD OF BUTTER. YOU CAN LITERALLY BAKE THIS BATTER IN ANY SHAPE OR FORM YOU (OR YOUR LITTLIES) WOULD LIKE. AS LONG AS THIS DOES NOT REPLACE NUTRIENT-DENSE VEGGIES AND CRUCIAL PROTEINS, IT CAN BE EATEN ONCE OR TWICE A DAY AS A SNACK OR AS PART OF A COMPLETE MEAL.

Sweetheart snacks

1 quantity Dough 8 (p. 30)

Prepare the dough as described in the recipe. Preheat the oven to 180 °C. Line a baking sheet with baking paper. Proceed according to the chosen recipe on pp. 140–141.

LEKKER TIP
Freeze little portions of sweetheart creations in zip-seal bags, just right for those grab-and-go days.

RECIPE	PORTIONS	TOTAL CARBS	FIBRE	NET CARBS	FAT	PROTEIN	KJ
Sandwiches	1	8 g	4.8 g	3.2 g	12 g	2.5 g	552
Shapes	1	6.4 g	3.9 g	2.5 g	9.6 g	2 g	444
Soft baby bagels	1	4.2 g	2.6 g	1.6 g	6.4 g	1.4 g	296
Apple rolls	1	8.1 g	4 g	4.1 g	10.7 g	2 g	508
Breadsticks	1	4.2 g	2.6 g	1.6 g	6.4 g	1.4 g	296
Custard slices	1	4.5 g	2.6 g	1.9 g	8.7 g	2.1 g	388

Sweetheart sandwiches

Take the chilled dough ball and roll out on the baking sheet until about 5 mm thick. Bake for 15–20 minutes or until golden. Allow to cool for a few minutes and then cut into squares, rectangles or thin circles using cookie cutters. Serve as is or spread with berry, apple or pear purée.

Yields 8 rectangular sandwiches

Sweetheart shapes

Take the chilled dough ball and roll out to about 1 cm thick on a plastic wrap-covered chopping board. Use your favourite set of cookie cutter shapes and press and lift with a blunt knife. Place on the prepared baking sheet pan. Re-roll the little offcuts until you have used up all the dough. Bake for 12–15 minutes until it just starts to brown. Allow it to cool and serve as is or with any of the dips in this chapter.

Yields 10 shapes

Sweetheart soft baby bagels and hearts

Take the chilled dough ball and roll into a 30 cm sausage. Cut into 15 pieces measuring 2 cm in length. Roll each piece into a sausage shape and tie the ends together to make bagel shapes. If making hearts, roll into slightly longer sausages and pinch the ends together in a heart shape. Place on the prepared baking sheet. Bake for 15–20 minutes or until golden. Allow to cool for a few minutes, then slice and serve with any spread from this chapter.

Yields 15 bagels

Sweetheart apple cinnamon rolls

Take the chilled dough ball and roll out to about 1 cm thick on a plastic wrap-covered chopping board. Spread ½ cup apple butter (or sugar-free apple sauce) over the sheet and sprinkle ½ cup fresh or frozen blueberries over the sauce. Dust lightly with ground cinnamon. Start at the bottom of the sheet and use the plastic wrap to help lift and roll up the dough. Cut into 2 cm-thick slices and arrange on the baking sheet, spaced apart to allow for expansion. Bake for 30–40 minutes.

Yields 12 rolls

Sweetheart breadsticks

Take the chilled dough ball and roll into a 30 cm sausage. Cut into 15 pieces measuring 2 cm in length. Roll each piece into a sausage shape, then cut in half for little hands to handle with ease. Place on the baking sheet. Bake for 10 minutes until just starting to brown (if it browns too much, it will end up being very hard upon cooling). Cool for a few minutes. Serve with any spread or dip from this chapter, mashed avocado or apple or berry sauce. The breadsticks also go well with soup or stew, and can be dipped into a soft-boiled egg for tots.

Yields 15 breadsticks

Sweetheart custard slices

This recipe uses egg yolks only and is suited for younger tummies, unless eggs seem to be an overall issue. Always consult a medical professional if you are uncertain about potential allergy symptoms.

Take the chilled dough ball and roll out on the baking sheet until about 5 mm thick. Bake for 15–20 minutes or until golden. Cool for a few minutes and then cut in half. Make ½ quantity Custard Filling (p. 169), using coconut cream instead of cream, and vanilla or cinnamon instead of lemon. Cool for 5 minutes. Spread the custard onto one sandwich layer and top with the remaining layer. Now cut into bite-size cubes, easy-to-handle strips or squares. It can be stored in the refrigerator for 2–3 days or freeze and thaw at room temperature.

Yields 16 slices

Meaty veg spread

RECIPE	PORTIONS	TOTAL CARBS	FIBRE	NET CARBS	FAT	PROTEIN	KJ
Meaty veg spread	¾ cup	13.8 g	6.2 g	7.6 g	23.4 g	23.9 g	1 428
Cheesy veg spread	¾ cup	14.5 g	6.2 g	8.3 g	40 g	17.6 g	1 916

½ cup mixed steamed veggies
½ cup cooked meat of choice
(chicken, chicken liver, beef mince,
tuna, lamb)
1 Broth Cube (p. 144) or ¼ cup
bone broth or coconut cream
1 Tbsp butter
1 Tbsp ground chia seeds (made in
a coffee grinder)
Herbs of choice

Purée all the ingredients together in a blender for a few seconds. It can be stored in the refrigerator for 2–3 days in an airtight container.

Yields ¾ cup

Cheesy veg spread
Follow the Meaty Veg Spread recipe, but replace the meat with the same quantity of cheese cubes.

Sunbutta nut-free spread

THIS IS A THICK, SPREADABLE NUT-FREE ALTERNATIVE TO PEANUT BUTTER AND OTHER NUT BUTTERS.

RECIPE	PORTIONS	TOTAL CARBS	FIBRE	NET CARBS	FAT	PROTEIN	KJ
Sunbutta spread	¾ cup	7.2 g	3 g	4.2 g	90.4 g	7.2 g	3 336
Chocbutta	¾ cup	9.1 g	4 g	5.1 g	90.9 g	7.8 g	3 368

¾ cup sunflower seeds
1 Tbsp xylitol
¼ tsp salt
⅓ cup melted coconut oil
½ tsp vanilla extract

Grind the sunflower seeds in a coffee grinder or blender – do this in two batches. Add all the ingredients to a blender and blend to a smooth, buttery consistency. Spoon into a glass jar and refrigerate until needed. Note that you need to leave the butta at room temperature for a little while after refrigeration to get a spreadable consistency again.

Yields ¾ cup

Chocbutta
Follow the Sunbutta recipe, but add 1–2 tsp cocoa powder plus an extra 1 tsp xylitol.

LEKKER TIP
Double this recipe and pour into a baking paper-lined square brownie pan. Refrigerate for a few hours until solid, lift out of the pan and cut into fudge-like blocks. This is more of a kiddie snack than a baby snack.

Apple cinnamon butta dip

RECIPE	PORTIONS	TOTAL CARBS	FIBRE	NET CARBS	FAT	PROTEIN	KJ
Apple butta dip	1	3.8 g	1.2 g	2.6 g	5.3 g	0.6 g	248

1 cup cubed apples (made from
steaming 2 cored and peeled
apples)
1 Tbsp butter
4–5 Tbsp coconut milk
1 Tbsp chia seeds
½ tsp ground cinnamon

Purée all the ingredients together in a blender for a few seconds. It can be stored in the refrigerator for 2–3 days in an airtight container.

Yields 4–6 portions

Berry butta dip

RECIPE	PORTIONS	TOTAL CARBS	FIBRE	NET CARBS	FAT	PROTEIN	KJ
Berry butta dip	¾ cup	28.1 g	7.8 g	20.3 g	28.4 g	3.6 g	1 424

½ cup cubed pears, steamed
½ cup blueberries, steamed
¼ cup coconut milk
1 Tbsp butter
1 Tbsp ground chia seeds (made in
a coffee grinder)

Purée all the ingredients together in a blender for a few seconds. It can be stored in the refrigerator for 2–3 days in an airtight container.

Yields ³/₄ cup

Broth cubes

RECIPE	PORTIONS	TOTAL CARBS	FIBRE	NET CARBS	FAT	PROTEIN	KJ
Broth cubes	1	<1 g	0 g	<1 g	0.7 g	0.5 g	28.8

Divide 1 cup bone broth into ice cube trays, then freeze and bag in zip-seal bags until required. Write the date on the bags.

Home-made super food jelly

RECIPE	PORTIONS	TOTAL CARBS	FIBRE	NET CARBS	FAT	PROTEIN	KJ
Super food jelly	1	2.7 g	0.3 g	2.4 g	0.5 g	7.1 g	880

3 Tbsp cold water
1 Tbsp gelatine powder
½ cup hot water
1 cup frozen blueberries or cored
and cubed apples or pears
½ tsp lemon juice (optional)
1 tsp vanilla extract
1–2 tsp xylitol, or to taste for older
kids (optional)

Place the cold water and the gelatine in a small bowl and allow to bloom for about 2 minutes. In a saucepan on medium-high heat, cook the berries/fruit in the hot water until tender. Add the lemon juice, vanilla and xylitol (if using). Place in a blender and blend for a few seconds. Add the bloomed gelatine to the hot berry/fruit purée and stir until completely dissolved. Pour into little silicone moulds and refrigerate for at least 2 hours until set. When serving, let your baby hold his or her own spoon to start experimenting with self-feeding techniques.

Yields 8–10 portions

LEKKER TIPS

- You can use strawberries, raspberries and blackberries instead of blueberries for older babies. When using blackberries or raspberries for younger children, purée them first and then press through a sieve before mixing into the jelly ingredients. They contain fibre that could be a bit harsh on little tummies.
- You can replace half of the hot water with ½ cup coconut cream. Just be sure to dissolve the bloomed gelatine into the hot half of the liquid before adding and blending the rest of the ingredients together.

TODDLERS
Mini sweet doughnut ooh-la-las

RECIPE	PORTIONS	TOTAL CARBS	FIBRE	NET CARBS	FAT	PROTEIN	KJ
Cinnamon sugar	1	2 g	0.8 g	1.6 g	4.5 g	1.6 g	200
Vanilla fudge glaze	1	1.8 g	0.2 g	1.6 g	5.3 g	1.7 g	228
Choc glaze	1	2 g	0.4 g	1.6 g	5.3 g	1.7 g	230
Vanilla icing	1	2.1 g	0.2 g	1.9 g	9.7 g	2 g	396
Lemon icing	1	2.1 g	0.2 g	1.9 g	9.7 g	2 g	396

1 quantity Sweet Mini Doughnuts
(Dough 7, sweet dough base, p. 28)

Prepare the doughnuts as described in the recipe and then add one or more of the following toppings and glazes.

CINNAMON SUGAR: Simply grind 2 Tbsp of xylitol in a coffee grinder and add some ground cinnamon to taste. Mix well and sprinkle over the doughnuts.

VANILLA FUDGE GLAZE
½ cup fresh cream
2 Tbsp butter
1–2 Tbsp xylitol (we prefer it less sweet)
1 tsp vanilla extract

Place all the ingredients in a saucepan on medium-high heat and boil and reduce for 3–5 minutes, whisking constantly. Don't let it get too thick or fudgy. Dip the mini doughnuts into the glaze.

CHOC GLAZE: Follow the Vanilla Fudge Glaze recipe, but omit the vanilla and add 1 heaped Tbsp cocoa powder instead.

VANILLA ICING
100 g cream cheese
100 g butter, at room temperature
¾ cup milk, fresh cream or coconut cream
Powdered xylitol to taste
1 tsp vanilla extract

Mix all the ingredients together until smooth. Scoop the icing on top of the doughnuts.

LEMON ICING: Follow the same recipe as Vanilla Icing, but omit the vanilla and add a squirt of lemon juice and some lemon zest.

LEKKER TIP
The Chocolate Glaze also makes a great sauce for waffles.

Cheesy mini doughnut bites with avo dip

RECIPE	PORTIONS	TOTAL CARBS	FIBRE	NET CARBS	FAT	PROTEIN	KJ
Cheesy bites	1	1.5 g	0.8 g	0.7 g	6.5 g	2.3 g	284

1 quantity Savoury Mini Doughnuts (Dough 7, savoury option 4 without the chilli, p. 28)
1 avocado
8 Tbsp coconut cream (optional)
Tiny pinch salt

Prepare the doughnuts as described in the recipe. Mash the avo, coconut cream and salt together. Serve the dip with the doughnuts.

Yields 36 bites

LEKKER TIP
These doughnuts are also wonderful dipped into a hearty soup or bolognaise meat sauce.

Mini doughnut sliders

THE KIDS WILL LOVE THE NOVELTY OF A DOUGHNUT HAMBURGER AND YOU GET TO SNEAK IN WONDERFUL FIBRE AND NUTRIENT-DENSE INGREDIENTS. THIS IS A GREAT RECIPE FOR LUNCHBOXES OR INSTANT MEALS. YOU CAN MAKE ALL OF THE COMPONENTS AHEAD OF TIME AND KEEP THEM FROZEN IN PORTIONS TO SUIT YOUR FAMILY. SLICE THE DOUGHNUTS BEFORE FREEZING – THIS WAY YOU CAN SIMPLY THAW, HEAT, FILL AND SERVE.

RECIPE	PORTIONS	TOTAL CARBS	FIBRE	NET CARBS	FAT	PROTEIN	KJ
Doughnut sliders	1	<1 g	0 g	<1 g	7.8 g	10.2 g	464

1 quantity Savoury Mini Doughnuts (Dough 7, savoury option 4 without the chilli, p. 28)
Your choice of mini hamburger patties, mini chicken fillet slices, bacon rashers cut into smaller pieces, tuna etc.
Carb-smart tomato sauce, mayonnaise or 1000 island sauce
Quartered real cheese slices, cream cheese or butter

Simply assemble your chosen ingredients to make these tiny sliders.

Yields 36 sliders

Berry pop-tarts

RECIPE	PORTIONS	TOTAL CARBS	FIBRE	NET CARBS	FAT	PROTEIN	KJ
Berry pop-tarts	1	11.5 g	5.8 g	5.7 g	13.3 g	4.7 g	684

FILLING

500 g frozen berries of choice

2 Tbsp xylitol

POP-TARTS

1 quantity Dough 3, made with

2 cups sunflower seed flour or

1 cup sunflower seed flour + 1 cup
nut flour (p. 18)

1 egg, beaten

TOPPING

1 quantity Royal Icing (p. 157) or
powdered xylitol

Place the berries and xylitol in a heavy-bottomed saucepan on medium heat and simmer for 15–20 minutes until reduced and a thicker, jam-like consistency. Allow to cool.

Preheat the oven to 180 °C. Line a baking sheet with baking paper.

Prepare the dough as described in the recipe. Take the chilled dough ball and roll out on a plastic wrap-covered chopping board until 5 mm thick. Use a round cookie cutter or drinking glass to cut out 16–20 circles from the dough sheet. Carefully lift and peel off the dough circles and place half of them onto the prepared baking sheet. Divide the cooled jam between the circles and top with the remaining half of the dough circles. Gently press down around the edges using a fork. Brush with the beaten egg and bake for 25–30 minutes until golden brown and puffed up.

Allow to cool, then top with royal icing or a dusting of xylitol.

Yields 8–10 pop-tarts

LEKKER TIPS

- Make the tarts a bit smaller and insert a popsicle stick into each to make cute pop-tart lollipops.
- Use any savoury filling of your choice or leftovers and grated cheese for a savoury version.

Sherbet

RECIPE	PORTIONS	TOTAL CARBS	FIBRE	NET CARBS	FAT	PROTEIN	KJ
Sherbet	1	0 g	0 g	0 g	0 g	0 g	230

2 Tbsp powdered xylitol (ground in
a coffee grinder)
¼ tsp each citric acid
¼ tsp tartaric acid
¼ tsp bicarbonate of soda
1 Caring Candies™ sugar-free
lollipop for dipping (optional)

Mix all the ingredients together. Use as is or grind in a coffee grinder
for a smooth powdered sherbet. Portion into two or more zip-seal
bags, or make pretty little cones with colourful paper and fill.

Yields 1 portion

> **LEKKER TIP**
> For fun, colourful sherbet replace the powdered xylitol with 2 Tbsp Simply delish natural jelly flavours.

Cheesy immune booster crackers

THESE CRACKERS ARE GREAT FOR TODDLERS AND OLDER CHILDREN. THE ADDITION OF TURMERIC BRIGHTENS THINGS UP AND GIVES AN IMMUNE BOOST AT THE SAME TIME.

RECIPE	PORTIONS	TOTAL CARBS	FIBRE	NET CARBS	FAT	PROTEIN	KJ
Cheesy crackers	1 cracker	1.8 g	1.2 g	0.6 g	4 g	1.6 g	256

1 quantity Dough 1 (with optional cheese if dairy can be tolerated, p. 14)
1 Tbsp finely chopped fresh herbs of choice and/or ½ tsp ground turmeric
1 egg, beaten (optional, if eggs can be tolerated)

Preheat the oven to 180 °C. Line a baking sheet with baking paper.

Prepare the dough as described in the recipe, adding the herbs to the dry ingredients before they are added to the butter-water mixture.

Take the chilled dough ball and roll out on the prepared baking sheet. Pre-cut the dough into squares (or use cookie cutters for different shapes). Brush lightly with the beaten egg if using and bake for 20–25 minutes.

Yields 32 squares

LEKKER TIPS
- You can play with many different herb or spice flavours and different types of cheese to turn this into an adventurous toddler snack. Parmesan will harden the batter slightly.
- Add a little tomato purée and oregano to the dough, then top with mozzarella to make little pizza bites.

Dairy-free lemon and berry popsicles

RECIPE	PORTIONS	TOTAL CARBS	FIBRE	NET CARBS	FAT	PROTEIN	KJ
Popsicles	1	5.7 g	1.6 g	4.1 g	9.8 g	1.2 g	460

1 cup frozen blueberries
1 cup frozen strawberries
2 Tbsp xylitol
6 Tbsp water
1 knifepoint debittered stevia
Juice and zest of 1 lemon
1 x 400 ml can coconut cream

Place the blueberries and strawberries in separate bowls. Add 1 Tbsp xylitol and 3 Tbsp water to each bowl of fruit. Add the stevia, lemon juice and zest to the coconut cream and stir well.

Place one bowl of fruit in a blender and blend until smooth. Pour the fruit purée into popsicle moulds, filling them one-third full. Pour the coconut cream mixture over the back of a spoon to fill another third of the popsicle moulds. Blend the remaining bowl of fruit until smooth. Fill the remaining third of the moulds with another layer of fruit purée. Freeze.

Yields 8–10 popsicles

Chocolate fudgesicles

A DELICIOUSLY CREAMY, SUPER FOOD, GUT-HEALING TREAT.

RECIPE	PORTIONS	TOTAL CARBS	FIBRE	NET CARBS	FAT	PROTEIN	KJ
Fudgesicles	1	6.2 g	1.9 g	4.3 g	17.2 g	3 g	740

½ Tbsp gelatine powder
2 Tbsp water
1 x 400 ml can coconut cream or
1½ cups fresh cream (if dairy is tolerated)
1–2 Tbsp cocoa powder
Pinch salt
2–3 Tbsp xylitol (optional, or sweeten to taste)
Few drops vanilla extract
3–4 blocks dark chocolate (85% cocoa solids), roughly chopped (optional)

Place the gelatine and water in a small bowl and allow the gelatine to bloom for a minute or two.

In a saucepan on medium heat, warm half of the coconut cream and then whisk in the cocoa, salt and xylitol. Add the gelatine to the warm coconut cream and stir until dissolved. Add the vanilla extract to the rest of the coconut cream. Chop the chocolate and sprinkle it into the tips of your popsicle moulds.

Add the cold vanilla cream to the warmer cocoa cream. Allow to cool a bit more before pouring into the moulds. Freeze.

Yields 6 fudgesicles

Jelly in my belly popsicles

RECIPE	PORTIONS	TOTAL CARBS	FIBRE	NET CARBS	FAT	PROTEIN	KJ
Jelly popsicles	1	3.9 g	0.7 g	3.2 g	8.2 g	3.2 g	400

1 cup boiling water
1 packet Simply delish natural jelly (any flavour)
½ x 400 ml can coconut cream or ¾ cup fresh cream
3 Tbsp amasi (optional probiotic booster)

Place the boiling water and jelly in a mixing bowl and stir for a few seconds until dissolved. Add the coconut cream and amasi, if using. Pour into popsicle moulds and freeze.

Yields 6 popsicles

> LEKKER TIP
> Double up this recipe and use two jelly flavours and the entire can of coconut cream. This way you will be stocked up during those summer heat waves.

Meringues

RECIPE	PORTIONS	TOTAL CARBS	FIBRE	NET CARBS	FAT	PROTEIN	KJ
Meringues	Entire batch	0.5 g	0 g	0.5 g	0.1 g	7.2 g	691

2 egg whites
1 Tbsp cool water
80 g powdered xylitol (ground in a coffee grinder)

Preheat the oven to 150 °C. Line two baking sheets with baking paper. Place the egg whites and water in the bowl of an electric mixer. Whisk on a low speed for about 1 minute, then increase the speed to medium and whisk for another 2–3 minutes or until the egg whites form stiff peaks. Add the xylitol 1 Tbsp at a time, until the mixture is stiff and glossy – this may take 5–10 minutes.

Spoon the meringue mixture into a piping bag and pipe ice cream cone-like swirls and cloud-like doodles onto the prepared baking sheets. Bake for 30–40 minutes or until the meringues are pale and dry. Switch off the oven and leave the fan on or leave the door ajar. Allow the meringues to cool and dry gradually in the oven.

Yields 12–24 meringues

LEKKER TIP

Use the piping bag to make butterflies, caterpillars or whatever your imagination can conjure up. Use a natural flavouring oil for fun flavours or sprinkle with some Simply delish natural jelly powder for a bit of colour.

Vanilla sun-flour cookies

RECIPE	PORTIONS	TOTAL CARBS	FIBRE	NET CARBS	FAT	PROTEIN	KJ
Vanilla cookies	1	0.9 g	0.3 g	0.6 g	6.4 g	1.4 g	300

2 cups sunflower seed flour (or
1 cup sunflower seed flour + 1 cup
nut flour of choice)
½ tsp salt
½ tsp bicarbonate of soda
125 g butter
¼ cup milk
2 Tbsp water
1 Tbsp gelatine powder
6 Tbsp xylitol
1 egg, beaten
½ tsp vanilla extract or 1 tsp vanilla
essence

Preheat the oven to 180 °C. Line a baking sheet with baking paper.

Place the flour, salt and bicarbonate of soda in a mixing bowl.

In a small saucepan on medium heat, warm the butter and milk until the butter has melted. Don't let the milk boil.

Place the water and gelatine in a small bowl and allow to bloom for a few minutes. Remove the milk mixture from heat and add the gelatine and xylitol. Stir with a whisk until well combined and completely dissolved. Add the gelatine mixture to the dry ingredients and start to mix. Add the beaten egg and vanilla and mix by hand until the dough comes together to form a ball. Place a sheet of plastic wrap on a cutting board and shape the dough into a sausage, using the sides of the plastic wrap to help shape the buttery, sticky dough. Wrap and allow the dough to set and chill in the freezer for a few minutes.

Remove the dough and slice into thin rounds. Sprinkle with a bit of xylitol (optional) and place on the prepared baking sheet. Alternatively, roll the dough into 2–3 cm balls, dip them in a bit of xylitol (optional) and arrange them on the baking sheet. Press with a fork to flatten slightly. Bake for 20–25 minutes.

Yields at least 24 cookies

Choc sandwich cookies

RECIPE	PORTIONS	TOTAL CARBS	FIBRE	NET CARBS	FAT	PROTEIN	KJ
Sandwich cookies	1	1.2 g	0.4 g	0.8 g	6.5 g	1.6 g	308

1 quantity Vanilla Sun-Flour
Cookies (see above)
2 slightly heaped Tbsp cocoa
powder
1 quantity Royal Icing (p. 157)

Preheat the oven to 180 °C. Line a baking sheet with baking paper.

Prepare the cookie dough as described in the recipe, adding the cocoa powder to the dry ingredients. Once the cookies have baked and cooled, sandwich them together with the royal icing.

Yields at least 24 cookies

Swirlies

RECIPE	PORTIONS	TOTAL CARBS	FIBRE	NET CARBS	FAT	PROTEIN	KJ
Swirlies	1	1.1 g	0.2 g	0.9 g	6.5 g	1.6 g	288

1 quantity Vanilla Sun-Flour Cookies dough (see opposite page)
1 quantity Choc Sandwich Cookies dough (see opposite page)

Preheat the oven to 180 °C. Line a baking sheet with baking paper.

Using a rolling pin, roll each chilled batter separately into a 5 mm-thick rectangle. (I roll mine between two sheets of plastic wrap: one wrapped around a chopping board and one on top of the dough.)

Place one rectangle on top of the other and trim the edges evenly. Use the plastic wrap to lift, compact and roll up the dough tightly from the bottom of the sheet to the top. Cut into thin rounds and space on the prepared baking sheet. Bake for 20–25 minutes.

Yields at least 48 cookies

The
sweet side

Christmas cookies ('Soetkoekies')

RECIPE	PORTIONS	TOTAL CARBS	FIBRE	NET CARBS	FAT	PROTEIN	KJ
Christmas cookies	Entire batch	23 g	7.9 g	15.1 g	154.4 g	31.3 g	6 272

2 cups sunflower seed flour (or
1 cup sunflower seed flour + 1 cup
nut flour of choice)
½ tsp salt
½ tsp bicarbonate of soda
125 g butter
¼ cup milk
1 egg, beaten
6 Tbsp xylitol
2 Tbsp water
1 Tbsp gelatine powder
1 tsp vanilla extract
Extra 2 Tbsp xylitol (optional)

ROYAL ICING
1 egg white
1 tsp vanilla extract
6 Tbsp powdered xylitol (grind in a
coffee grinder)

Preheat the oven to 180 °C. Line a baking sheet with baking paper.

Place the flour, salt and bicarbonate of soda in a mixing bowl.

In a small saucepan on medium heat, warm the butter and milk until the butter has melted. Don't let the milk boil.

In a separate bowl, whisk the egg and xylitol together until creamy.

Place the water and gelatine in a small bowl and allow to bloom. Remove milk mix from heat and add the gelatine. Stir with a whisk until well combined and completely dissolved. Add the gelatine mixture to the dry ingredients and start to mix. Add the beaten egg and vanilla and mix by hand until the dough comes together to form a dense, elastic ball (it will appear smooth and glossy). Roll pieces of dough into 2–3 cm balls, dip them in xylitol if using and place them on the prepared baking sheet. Press with the base of a glass to form 4–5 mm-thick, round cookies. Bake for 20–25 minutes. Cool (these cookies will harden upon cooling).

For the icing, use an electric mixer to beat the egg white and vanilla until frothy. Slowly add the xylitol and beat on a slower speed until stiff peaks form and the icing has a glossy appearance. This should take 5–7 minutes. Place the icing into a piping bag (or small plastic bag with the corner snipped off) and decorate your cookies to your heart's content. Alternatively, just spread a solid layer of icing onto each cookie. Allow the icing to air-dry and harden a bit before serving.

Yields at least 36 cookies

LEKKER TIPS

- This batter is also perfect for cookie cutter shapes. Place the dough on a plastic wrap-covered surface and place another sheet of plastic wrap over the dough (this will prevent the dough sticking to the rolling pin). Using a rolling pin, roll out the dough until about 5 mm thick. Remove the top sheet of plastic wrap and cut out shapes. Bake on a baking paper-lined baking sheet until golden brown.
- For a lemon cream cookie, simply place the dough ball on a sheet of plastic wrap and mould it into a sausage the diameter you would like the cookies to be. Wrap in the plastic wrap and allow to set in the freezer for 5–10 minutes. Slice into 5 mm-thick rounds and place on the prepared baking sheet. Use a cookie stencil with a pattern or simply prick with a fork. Bake for 15 minutes or until cookies are golden brown around the edges. Cool. Make a batch of royal icing and replace the vanilla with the same quantity of lemon oil or essence or 1 Tbsp lemon juice and zest of 1 lemon. Sandwich the cookies together with the icing.
- For an even harder cookie, try baking these with erythritol instead of xylitol. It works like a charm.

Old-fashioned aniseed rusks

RECIPE	PORTIONS	TOTAL CARBS	FIBRE	NET CARBS	FAT	PROTEIN	KJ
Aniseed rusks	1 rusk	1.7 g	0.8 g	0.9 g	5.8 g	1.6 g	240

1½ cups coconut meal (made from desiccated coconut ground in a coffee grinder)
1 cup nut flour
½ tsp bicarbonate of soda
1 tsp baking powder
1 Tbsp ground chia seeds (ground in a coffee grinder)
1 slightly heaped Tbsp anise seeds
2–3 Tbsp xylitol
½ tsp salt
1 Tbsp apple cider vinegar
4 eggs
½ cup melted butter or coconut oil
½ cup milk or coconut milk

Preheat the oven to 180 °C. Line one large rectangular pan or two loaf pans with baking paper.

Mix the coconut meal, flour, bicarbonate of soda, baking powder, ground chia seeds, anise seeds, xylitol and salt together in a bowl.

In a separate bowl, whisk the vinegar, eggs, melted butter and milk together and mix well. Add the wet ingredients to the dry ingredients, mixing for a minute in order for the dough to settle.

Pour the batter into the prepared pan(s). Dip your hand in some milk and smooth the top of the batter gently. Bake for 30 minutes or until baked through and nicely browned on top.

Allow to cool before you cut it into 1.5 cm-thick slices. Cut each slice in half.

Turn the oven down to 150 °C and place the rusk slices directly on to a wired rack. Dry for 1 hour, turning halfway through. Store in an airtight container.

Yields 36–40 rusks

Old-fashioned spice cookies

RECIPE	PORTIONS	TOTAL CARBS	FIBRE	NET CARBS	FAT	PROTEIN	KJ
Spice cookies	Entire batch	27.9 g	11.1 g	16.8 g	154.8 g	28 g	6 276

2 cups sunflower seed flour (or
1 cup sunflower seed flour + 1 cup
nut flour of choice)
½ tsp ground mixed spice
½ tsp ground cinnamon
½ tsp ground cloves
½ tsp salt
½ tsp bicarbonate of soda
125 g butter
¼ cup milk
2 Tbsp water
1 Tbsp gelatine powder
6 Tbsp xylitol
1 egg, beaten
1 tsp vanilla extract

FOR DIPPING
2 Tbsp xylitol (optional)
1 tsp ground cinnamon

Preheat the oven to 180 °C. Line a baking sheet with baking paper.
Place the flour, spices, salt and bicarbonate of soda in a bowl.
In a small saucepan on medium heat, warm the butter and milk until the butter has melted. Don't let the milk boil.
Place the water and gelatine in a small bowl and allow to bloom for a few minutes. Remove milk mix from heat and add the gelatine and xylitol. Stir with a whisk until well combined and completely dissolved. Add the gelatine mixture to the dry ingredients and start to mix. Add the beaten egg and vanilla and mix by hand until the dough comes together to form a ball. Roll pieces of dough into 2–3 cm balls, dip them in xylitol and cinnamon and place them on the prepared baking sheet. Press with the base of a glass and bake for 20–25 minutes. Cool.

Yields at least 36 cookies

LEKKER TIP
You can decorate these with pretty patterns using Royal Icing (p. 157).

Coffee sandwich cookies

RECIPE	PORTIONS	TOTAL CARBS	FIBRE	NET CARBS	FAT	PROTEIN	KJ
Coffee cookies	Entire batch	22.3 g	7.9 g	14.4 g	154.4 g	27.8 g	6 156

2 cups sunflower seed flour (or
1 cup sunflower seed flour + 1 cup
nut flour of choice)
½ tsp salt
½ tsp bicarbonate of soda
125 g butter
3 Tbsp strong instant coffee
granules
¼ cup milk
2 Tbsp water
1 Tbsp gelatine powder
6 Tbsp xylitol
1 egg, beaten
1 tsp vanilla extract

COFFEE-FLAVOURED ROYAL ICING
2 tsp instant coffee powder
6 Tbsp xylitol
1 egg white
1 tsp vanilla extract

Preheat the oven to 180 °C. Line a baking sheet with baking paper.

Place the flour, salt and bicarbonate of soda in a mixing bowl.

In a small saucepan on medium heat, warm the butter, coffee granules and milk until the butter has melted. Don't let the milk boil.

Place the water and gelatine in a small bowl and allow to bloom for a few minutes. Remove milk mix from heat and add the gelatine and xylitol. Stir with a whisk until well combined and completely dissolved. Add the gelatine mixture to the dry ingredients and start to mix. Add the beaten egg and vanilla and mix by hand until the dough comes together to form a ball.

Roll out the dough on the prepared baking sheet and then cut into 2 x 6 cm strips or whatever rectangular size fits your pan's dimensions best (you are aiming to make a long, 'dunkable' sandwich cookie). Alternatively, pinch off pieces of dough and gently roll into a finger shape. Space out on the baking sheet and press down with a fork. Bake for 20–25 minutes.

While the dough is still warm, remove from the pan and cut again over the pre-cut lines. These cookies harden upon cooling.

For the icing, grind the instant coffee powder and xylitol in a coffee grinder. Use an electric mixer to beat the egg white and vanilla until frothy. Slowly add the xylitol-coffee mixture and beat on a lower speed until stiff peaks form and the icing has a glossy appearance. This should take 5–7 minutes. Sandwich cookies together with the icing and allow to air-dry a bit before packing into an airtight container.

Yields at least 36 cookies

Hertzoggies

RECIPE	PORTIONS	TOTAL CARBS	FIBRE	NET CARBS	FAT	PROTEIN	KJ
Hertzoggies	1 jam tart	4.6 g	2.3 g	2.3 g	11 g	2.5 g	484

BASE

1 quantity Dough 6, Sweet Pie Crust (p. 24)

FILLING

500 g frozen strawberries
2 Tbsp xylitol

MERINGUE TOPPING

3 egg whites
6 Tbsp powdered xylitol (ground in a coffee grinder)
1¼ cups desiccated coconut

Preheat the oven to 180 °C. Grease two 12-hole regular cupcake pans.

Prepare the pie crust batter as described in the recipe.

For the filling, place the strawberries and xylitol in a saucepan on medium heat and simmer gently for 15–20 minutes until reduced to a thicker, jam-like consistency. Allow to cool.

Press the dough about halfway up the sides of the cupcake moulds and smooth the edges a bit (I use a silicone cupcake pan as it is much easier to pop these out after baking). Bake for 5–7 minutes.

For the meringue topping, use an electric mixer to whisk the egg whites until they start to form stiff peaks. Add the xylitol bit by bit as you continue to mix. As soon as all the xylitol is incorporated and the meringue has a glossy appearance, stir in the coconut.

Allow the dough cups to cool slightly for a minute or two, and then scoop in a heaped teaspoon of jam filling followed by the coconut meringue topping. Bake for 15–20 minutes until brown and set.

Yields 24 jam tarts

LEKKER TIP

You could use the same ratios to make the original apricot jam filling, but the strawberry filling is a lower carb option and looks really pretty too. You can also assemble all the jam tarts in advance and then bake – it is a bit of a time saver and still yields a lovely, slightly moist tartlet.

Millionaire's Shortbread

RECIPE	PORTIONS	TOTAL CARBS	FIBRE	NET CARBS	FAT	PROTEIN	KJ
Shortbread	1 large square	7 g	3.6 g	3.4 g	35 g	4.7 g	1 380
Shortbread	1 small square	1.8 g	0.9 g	0.9 g	8.8 g	1.2 g	344

BASE
1 quantity Dough 6, Sweet Pie Crust (p. 24)

BASIC CARAMEL SAUCE
6 Tbsp butter
3 Tbsp xylitol
1 cup fresh cream

CHOCOLATE LAYER
¼ cup coconut oil
3 Tbsp xylitol
¼ cup coconut cream
¼ cup cocoa powder

Preheat the oven to 180 °C. Line a 23 cm x 33 cm baking sheet with baking paper.

Prepare the pie crust batter as described in the recipe. Press the dough directly onto the prepared baking sheet and use a rolling pin to smooth it out. Bake for 15–20 minutes or until slightly browned and set. Allow to cool.

For the caramel layer, melt the butter in a saucepan on medium heat. Add the xylitol and stir with a whisk to dissolve. Slowly add the cream. Let it simmer and bubble, while whisking, for 10–12 minutes. The caramel is ready when it is thick and glossy and slower bursting bubbles appear. Pour the caramel over the cooled base and pop it into the fridge while you make the chocolate layer.

For the chocolate layer, melt the coconut oil in a saucepan on medium heat. Add the xylitol and stir with a whisk to dissolve. Add the coconut cream and cocoa powder. Whisk and simmer for about 3 minutes – it will thicken suddenly. Gently whisk for another 20 seconds and then remove from heat. Pour the slightly cooled chocolate over the caramel layer and place in the freezer for 30–60 minutes.

Using a very sharp knife, cut it into your desired portions. Serve and store what you are not using right away in the freezer. (They are actually amazingly good eaten frozen.)

Yields 10 large squares or 40 small squares

LEKKER TIP
Add a few drops of mint oil to the melted chocolate to transform these into after-dinner mint treats. Listen properly: it will be seven billion eight hundred million thousand and twenty hundred times worth the trouble!

Tiramisu

RECIPE	PORTIONS	TOTAL CARBS	FIBRE	NET CARBS	FAT	PROTEIN	KJ
Tiramisu	1 block	5.4 g	0.6 g	4.8 g	21.4 g	10.2 g	1 054
Tiramisu	1 ramekin	6.2 g	1 g	5.2 g	27.8 g	11.5 g	1 316

CREAM FILLING
6 eggs, separated
¼ cup xylitol
2 x 250 g tubs mascarpone cheese

COOKIE LAYERS
1 cup strong brewed coffee
¼ cup rum (optional)
1 Tbsp xylitol
1 quantity Christmas Cookies
(p. 157), rolled and baked into
round or elongated finger-length
cookies

TOPPING
2–3 blocks dark chocolate (80%
cocoa solids)

For the cream filling, beat the egg yolks and xylitol for at least 15 minutes or until thick and white. Add the mascarpone and beat until just combined but smooth.

For the cookie layers, combine the coffee, rum and 1 Tbsp xylitol in a bowl. Quickly dip the cookies into the liquid and set aside on a dinner plate.

Beat the egg whites until thick and stiff peaks form, and gently fold into the mascarpone cream mixture.

Layer the soaked biscuits and mascarpone cream in a large glass bowl or ramekins, ending with a layer of the cream. Refrigerate overnight or for at least 2–3 hours.

Place the chocolate blocks in the freezer. Break the frozen blocks into smaller chunks and grind into a lovely chocolate powder using your coffee grinder (or simply grate the chocolate).

Before serving, top the tiramisu generously with grated chocolate.

Yields 12 portioned blocks or 8 ramekins or glass bowl portions

Crème brûlée

RECIPE	PORTIONS	TOTAL CARBS	FIBRE	NET CARBS	FAT	PROTEIN	KJ
Crème brûlée	1	3.1 g	0 g	3.1 g	8.9 g	3.3 g	424

2 cups fresh double cream
½ tsp vanilla extract
2 Tbsp xylitol for cream mixture
and extra xylitol for sprinkling
6 egg yolks

Preheat the oven to 160 °C. You will need six ramekins.

Pour the cream into a saucepan. Add the vanilla. Bring the cream to boiling point, then reduce the heat and simmer gently for 5 minutes.

Meanwhile, in a large heatproof bowl, beat the 2 Tbsp xylitol and egg yolks together until light in colour and fluffy in texture.

Bring the cream back to boiling point. Pour it over the egg mixture, whisking continuously, until thickened somewhat. Fill the ramekins to about two-thirds full.

Place the ramekins into a large roasting tray and pour in enough hot water to come halfway up the sides. Place onto the centre shelf of the oven and bake for 40–45 minutes, or until the custard is just set but still a bit wobbly in the centre. Remove the ramekins from the water and set aside to cool to room temperature, then chill until needed.

When ready to serve, sprinkle 1 heaped tsp xylitol (or a bit more...) evenly over the surface of each crème brûlée, then caramelise under the grill for a few minutes or use a chef's blowtorch.

Yields 6 portions

NOTE
This recipe does not make the hard cap that regular sugar would achieve. Xylitol cannot harden like sugar, BUT the taste is a perfect marriage between creamy, smooth custard and a slightly burnt sweet topping.

Lemon sherbet macaroons

RECIPE	PORTIONS	TOTAL CARBS	FIBRE	NET CARBS	FAT	PROTEIN	KJ
Lemon macaroons	1 macaroon	3.9 g	1.6 g	2.3 g	6.6 g	1.7 g	312

2 cups desiccated coconut
1 Tbsp xylitol
¼ tsp debittered stevia powder
Zest and juice of 1 medium lemon
4 large egg whites
50 g dark chocolate (85% cocoa solids, optional)

Preheat the oven to 190 °C. Line one or two baking sheets with baking paper.

Mix the coconut, xylitol, stevia, lemon zest and juice together in a mixing bowl. Use an electric mixer to beat the egg whites until stiff peaks form. Use a rubber spatula to fold the egg whites into the coconut mixture.

Use two tablespoons to form the mixture into compact clusters and place on the prepared baking sheet(s). Bake for 20–25 minutes until the tops are lightly golden and the bottoms and edges are deeply golden.

If dipping the macaroons in chocolate, melt the chocolate in a double boiler over simmering water. Dip the bottoms of the macaroons into the chocolate, letting any excess drip back into the bowl, and return to the lined baking sheets. Place the macaroons in the refrigerator for about 10 minutes to allow the chocolate to set. The cookies keep well in an airtight container at room temperature for 3–4 days.

Yields 18–20 macaroons

Lemon sherbet macaroon tartlets

RECIPE	PORTIONS	TOTAL CARBS	FIBRE	NET CARBS	FAT	PROTEIN	KJ
Macaroon tartlets	1 tartlet	4.9 g	2.3 g	2.6 g	12.2 g	4.4 g	564

TARTLET SHELLS
1 quantity Lemon Sherbet Macaroon mixture (see opposite page)

LEMON CUSTARD FILLING
3 Tbsp cold milk or water
1 Tbsp gelatine powder
1 cup fresh cream or coconut cream
6 egg yolks
3 Tbsp xylitol
Juice and zest of 1 lemon

For the shells, preheat the oven to 180 °C. Set out 10–12 tartlet moulds or silicone muffin cups.

Prepare the macaroon mixture as described in the recipe. Scoop a heaped tablespoon of the mixture into each mould or muffin cup and compact it in the same way you would line a pie with crust. Bake for 15–20 minutes until the edges are lightly golden and the bottoms start to turn golden too. Allow to cool.

For the custard, combine the milk and gelatine in a small bowl and allow to bloom for a few minutes.

Slowly heat the cream in a medium saucepan until just warm, not boiling.

In a separate mixing bowl, whisk the egg yolks and xylitol. Whisk the lukewarm cream into the egg mixture and pour back into the saucepan. Now, on low heat, stir the custard with a wooden spoon and add the lemon juice and zest. Stir for a good few minutes until the custard thickens to a pouring consistency.

Remove from heat, whisk in the gelatine and allow the custard to cool to room temperature. Pour the custard into the macaroon crusts and refrigerate. The custard will set once chilled.

Yields 10–12 tartlets

Orange chocolate macaroon tartlets

RECIPE	PORTIONS	TOTAL CARBS	FIBRE	NET CARBS	FAT	PROTEIN	KJ
Macaroon tartlets	1 tartlet	5.8 g	2.6 g	3.2 g	12.2 g	4.5 g	576

TARTLET SHELLS

2 cups desiccated coconut

2 Tbsp cocoa powder

1 Tbsp xylitol

¼ tsp debittered stevia powder

Zest and juice of ½ medium orange

4 large egg whites

CHOCOLATE CUSTARD FILLING

3 Tbsp cold milk or water

1 Tbsp gelatine powder

1 cup fresh cream or coconut cream

6 egg yolks

2 Tbsp cocoa powder

3 Tbsp xylitol

2–3 Tbsp orange juice

1 tsp vanilla extract

For the shells, preheat the oven to 180 °C. Set out 10–12 tartlet moulds or silicone muffin cups.

Mix the coconut, cocoa powder, xylitol, stevia, orange zest and juice together in a mixing bowl. Use an electric mixer to beat the egg whites until stiff peaks form. Use a rubber spatula to fold the egg whites into the coconut mixture.

Scoop a heaped tablespoon of the mixture into each mould or muffin cup and compact it in the same way you would line a pie dish with crust. Bake for 15–20 minutes until the edges are lightly golden and the bottoms start to turn golden too. Allow to cool.

For the custard, combine the milk and gelatine in a small bowl and allow to bloom for a few minutes.

Slowly heat the cream in a medium saucepan until just warm, not boiling.

In a separate mixing bowl, whisk the egg yolks, cocoa and xylitol. Whisk the lukewarm cream into the egg mixture and pour back into the saucepan. Now, on low heat, stir the custard with a wooden spoon and add the orange juice and vanilla. Stir for a good few minutes until the custard thickens to a pouring consistency.

Remove from heat, whisk in the gelatine and allow the custard to cool to room temperature. Pour the custard into the macaroon crusts and refrigerate. The custard will set once chilled.

Yields 10–12 tartlets

Espresso custard macaroon tartlets

RECIPE	PORTIONS	TOTAL CARBS	FIBRE	NET CARBS	FAT	PROTEIN	KJ
Macaroon tartlets	1 tartlet	4.4 g	2.2 g	2.2 g	12.1 g	4.2 g	552

TARTLET SHELLS
2 cups desiccated coconut
1 Tbsp xylitol
¼ tsp debittered stevia powder
2 Tbsp freshly ground coffee beans
4 large egg whites

ESPRESSO CUSTARD FILLING
3 Tbsp cold milk or water
1 Tbsp gelatine powder
1 cup fresh cream or coconut cream
6 egg yolks
3 Tbsp xylitol
1 tsp vanilla extract
1–2 Tbsp espresso instant coffee dissolved in 1–2 Tbsp warm water

For the shells, preheat the oven to 180 °C. Set out 10–12 tartlet moulds or silicone muffin cups.

Mix the coconut, xylitol, stevia and freshly ground coffee beans together in a mixing bowl. Use an electric mixer to beat the egg whites until stiff peaks form. Use a rubber spatula to fold the egg whites into the coconut mixture.

Scoop a heaped tablespoon of the mixture into each mould or muffin cup and compact it in the same way you would line a pie dish with crust. Bake for 15–20 minutes until the edges are lightly golden and the bottoms start to turn golden too. Allow to cool.

For the custard, combine the milk and gelatine in a small bowl and allow to bloom for a few minutes.

Slowly heat the cream in a medium saucepan until just warm, not boiling.

In a separate mixing bowl, whisk the egg yolks and xylitol. Whisk the lukewarm cream into the egg mixture and pour back into the saucepan. Now, on low heat, stir the custard with a wooden spoon and add the vanilla and coffee. Stir for a good few minutes until the custard thickens to a pouring consistency.

Remove from heat, whisk in the gelatine and allow the custard to cool to room temperature. Pour the custard into the macaroon crusts and refrigerate. The custard will set once chilled.

Yields 10–12 tartlets

Rooibos chai macaroon tartlets

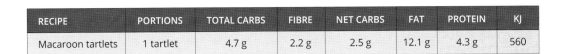

RECIPE	PORTIONS	TOTAL CARBS	FIBRE	NET CARBS	FAT	PROTEIN	KJ
Macaroon tartlets	1 tartlet	4.7 g	2.2 g	2.5 g	12.1 g	4.3 g	560

TARTLET SHELLS
2 cups desiccated coconut
¼ tsp debittered stevia powder
1–2 rooibos tea bags
1 Tbsp xylitol
4 large egg whites

CHAI CUSTARD FILLING
3 Tbsp cold milk or water
1 Tbsp gelatine powder
1 cup fresh cream or coconut cream
4 rooibos chai tea bags
¼ tsp ground cardamom
¼ tsp ground cinnamon
Pinch ground cloves
6 egg yolks
3 Tbsp xylitol

For the shells, preheat the oven to 180 °C. Set out 10–12 tartlet moulds or silicone muffin cups.

Mix the coconut and stevia together in a mixing bowl. Tear the corners off the tea bags and grind the tea leaves and xylitol together in a coffee grinder. Add to the coconut mixture. Use an electric mixer to beat the egg whites until stiff peaks form. Use a rubber spatula to fold the egg whites into the coconut mixture.

Scoop a heaped tablespoon of the mixture into each mould or muffin cup and compact it in the same way you would line a pie dish with crust. Bake for 15–20 minutes until the edges are lightly golden and the bottoms start to turn golden too. Allow to cool.

For the custard, combine the milk and gelatine in a small bowl and allow to bloom for a few minutes.

Slowly heat the cream, chai tea bags and spices in a medium saucepan until just warm, not boiling.

In a separate mixing bowl, whisk the egg yolks and xylitol. Remove the tea bags from the cream mixture and whisk the lukewarm cream into the egg mixture. Pour back into the saucepan. Now, on low heat, stir the custard with a wooden spoon. Stir for about 5 minutes until the custard thickens to a pouring consistency.

Remove from heat, whisk in the gelatine and allow the custard to cool to room temperature. Pour the custard into the macaroon crusts and refrigerate. The custard will set once chilled.

Yields 10–12 tartlets

LEKKER TIP

Sandwich two tartlets together with whipped cream, freeze for 30–60 minutes and get ready to fall in love! For a dairy-free version, use coconut cream in the custard, then whip ice-cold coconut cream in an electric mixer until stiff and sandwich two tartlets together.

Lemon custard fruity tartlets

BAKE THE TARTLET SHELLS USING EITHER FOIL PANS IN THE SIZE YOU PREFER, STANDARD SILICONE MUFFIN CUPS (SHELL PRESSED HALFWAY UP THE SIDES) OR SMALL QUICHE PANS. I HAVE USED VERY SMALL MUFFIN MOULDS FOR CATERING PURPOSES TOO. JUST ADJUST BAKING TIMES ACCORDINGLY.

RECIPE	PORTIONS	TOTAL CARBS	FIBRE	NET CARBS	FAT	PROTEIN	KJ
With fresh berries	1 tartlet	6.7 g	2.7 g	4 g	19 g	5.6 g	840
With berry compote	1 tartlet	7.8 g	2.9 g	4.9 g	20 g	5.8 g	900
With berry cream	1 tartlet	6.7 g	2.6 g	4.1 g	20.6 g	5.7 g	904

1 quantity Dough 6, Sweet Pie Crust (p. 24)
1 quantity Lemon Custard Filling (p. 169)

Prepare the pie crust batter and bake the tartlet shells as described in the recipe.

Prepare the filling as described in the recipe and pour into the cooled tartlet shells. Top with one of the following options.

TOPPING OPTION 1: FRESH BERRIES
Slice (or leave whole, depending on size) 1½ cups fresh berries of choice and arrange on top of the freshly poured custard. Chill and serve with a dusting of powdered xylitol and garnish with fresh mint and lavender.

Yields 24 standard cupcake-size tartlets

TOPPING OPTION 2: BERRY COMPOTE
In a saucepan on medium heat, warm 2 cups frozen berries of choice along with 1–2 Tbsp xylitol and 3 Tbsp water. Allow the berries to simmer in their own juices for 5–6 minutes. Pour the compote into a serving dish with a spoon and allow guests to scoop the desired amount of compote onto the tartlets. Add a dollop of whipped cream for decadence.

Yields 24 standard cupcake-size tartlets

TOPPING OPTION 3: BERRY-INFUSED CREAM
In a saucepan on medium heat, warm ½ cup frozen berries of choice along with 2 tsp xylitol and 1 Tbsp water. Allow the berries to simmer in their own juices for about 3 minutes and reduce to a syrup. Purée the berries in a blender and stir into 1½–2 cups fresh cream. Whip the cream with the berries and scoop dollops onto the tartlets. Garnish with fresh berries or mint leaves.

Yields 24 standard cupcake-size tartlets

Choc-caramel cream pie

RECIPE	PORTIONS	TOTAL CARBS	FIBRE	NET CARBS	FAT	PROTEIN	KJ
Cream pie	1 slice	6.6 g	2.1 g	4.5 g	21 g	4.7 g	900

1 quantity Dough 6, Sweet Pie Crust (p. 24)
1 quantity Chocolate Custard Filling (p. 170)
1 quantity Caramel Sauce (p. 165)
1 cup whipped fresh cream (optional)
2 blocks dark chocolate (85% cocoa solids), grated (optional)

Prepare the pie crust batter as described in the recipe and bake the crusts in two foil pans.

Prepare the filling as described in the recipe and pour into the cooled tartlet shells. Refrigerate until the filling has set.

Prepare the caramel sauce as described in the recipe. Allow to cool and then whip the sauce to a spreading consistency. Spread over the chocolate custard filling. Spread or pipe the whipped cream over the caramel layer and sprinkle with some grated chocolate.

Yields 16 slices

> **LEKKER TIP**
> Add a few drops of mint oil to the chocolate custard to give any peppermint tart a run for its money!

No-bake raspberry–choc cheesecake

RECIPE	PORTIONS	TOTAL CARBS	FIBRE	NET CARBS	FAT	PROTEIN	KJ
Cheesecake	1 portion	7.5 g	2.4 g	5.1 g	32 g	7.1 g	1 356

CHEESECAKE FILLING
1 Tbsp gelatine powder
3 Tbsp water
2 cups frozen raspberries
¼ cup xylitol
2 x 250 g tubs creamed cottage cheese
½ tub or 125 g crème fraîche
2 tsp vanilla extract

CHOCOLATE GANACHE
2 Tbsp coconut oil
½ tub or 125 g crème fraîche
2 Tbsp xylitol
2 Tbsp cocoa powder

For the filling, combine the gelatine and water in a small bowl and allow to bloom for 2–3 minutes.

In a saucepan on medium-high heat, warm the raspberries and xylitol and simmer for 2–3 minutes until reduced. Add the gelatine and stir to dissolve. Cool slightly and then combine with all the remaining filling ingredients. Mix until well combined.

For the ganache, melt the coconut oil in a saucepan on medium-high heat, and then add the rest of the ingredients. Whisk for a minute or so until all the ingredients are combined and thick (this sauce thickens quite quickly). Remove from heat as soon as it thickens.

Use 6–8 pretty glasses, such as wine or whiskey glasses, and fill with a layer of cheesecake filling, followed by a thin layer of ganache. Chill for 1 hour and serve garnished with a couple of fresh berries, mint leaves or dark chocolate curls.

Yields 6–8 slices

Pumpkin and rooibos mini cheesecakes

RECIPE	PORTIONS	TOTAL CARBS	FIBRE	NET CARBS	FAT	PROTEIN	KJ
Mini cheesecake	1 cheesecake	9.8 g	3 g	6.8 g	19.8 g	13.7 g	888

BASE

½ quantity Old-fashioned Spice
Cookies (p. 160), about 8 cm in
diameter (keep the rest for lunchboxes)

ROOIBOS JELLY

1 Tbsp gelatine powder
2 Tbsp cold water
6 vanilla rooibos tea bags
2 cups boiling water
¼ cup xylitol

CHEESECAKE FILLING

2 Tbsp gelatine powder
6 Tbsp water
2 cups cooked, drained and
mashed pumpkin
2 tsp vanilla extract
1 slightly heaped Tbsp ground
cinnamon
¼ cup xylitol
2 x 250 g tubs creamed
cottage cheese
½ tub or 125 g crème fraîche

For the base, prepare the biscuits as described in the recipe. Grease eight large cupcake silicone moulds.

For the rooibos jelly, combine the gelatine and cold water in a small bowl and allow to bloom for a few minutes. Steep the tea bags in the boiling water for a few minutes. Remove the tea bags and add the xylitol and gelatine. Stir until dissolved. Pour equal amounts into the prepared moulds, arranged on a baking sheet. Refrigerate for about 30 minutes until fairly set.

For the filling, combine the gelatine and water in a small bowl and allow to bloom for 2–3 minutes. In a saucepan on medium heat, warm the pumpkin, vanilla, cinnamon and xylitol and simmer gently for 1 minute. Add the gelatine to the pumpkin mixture and stir to dissolve. Remove from heat and allow to cool slightly.

In a large mixing bowl, combine all the rest of the filling ingredients along with the cooled pumpkin mixture. Mix until well combined. Scoop eight equal amounts on top of the rooibos jelly in the moulds and place a spice cookie on top of the filling. Allow to set for 1 hour or overnight. Using a sharp knife, cut around the edges of the silicone mould and tip the mini cheesecake out onto a serving dish. The cookie will form the bottom crust of the cheesecake with a lovely see-through jelly layer on top.

Yields 8 mini cheesecakes

LEKKER TIP

This dessert can be deconstructed and you can use only some of the elements. It is lovely served in pretty glasses with the cookie acting as a wafer, or just do a cheesecake layer in a cup and add the rooibos jelly on top. Allow to set and serve.

Orange and dark chocolate biscotti

RECIPE	PORTIONS	TOTAL CARBS	FIBRE	NET CARBS	FAT	PROTEIN	KJ
Biscotti	1 biscotti	3.3 g	1.3 g	2 g	10.4 g	2.9 g	448

1 cup nut flour
1 cup sunflower seed flour
1 Tbsp ground chia seeds (ground in a coffee grinder)
2 tsp baking powder
½ cup flaked almonds
3–4 blocks Lindt dark chocolate (85% cocoa solids), chopped
2 eggs
¼ cup xylitol
½ cup butter, melted
2 tsp vanilla extract
½ tsp almond extract (optional)
Zest of 1 orange
1 egg white, lightly beaten

Preheat the oven to 180 °C. Line a baking sheet with baking paper.

In a mixing bowl, combine the flours, ground chia seeds, baking powder, almonds and choc chips.

In a separate bowl, whisk the eggs, xylitol, butter, vanilla, almond extract and orange zest. Stir the wet ingredients into the dry ingredients until a soft, sticky dough forms. Transfer to a lightly floured surface and form into a smooth ball. Divide the dough in half and roll each half into a 30 cm-long log. Transfer to the baking sheet. Brush the tops with egg white, then bake for 20 minutes. Remove from oven and cool on a wire rack for 5 minutes. Turn the oven down to 160 °C. Transfer each log to a cutting board and cut diagonally into 1.5 cm-thick slices. Stand the cookies upright on the baking sheet and return to the oven for 25–30 minutes. Transfer to a wire rack to cool.

Yields 18–20 biscotti

Chocolate lime soufflé

RECIPE	PORTIONS	TOTAL CARBS	FIBRE	NET CARBS	FAT	PROTEIN	KJ
Chocolate soufflé	1	10.2 g	2.2 g	8 g	37 g	9.5 g	1 658

1 Tbsp butter and 1 Tbsp cocoa for greasing and dusting ramekins
80–100g dark chocolate (85% cocoa solids)
80 g butter or coconut oil
¾ cup fresh cream or coconut cream
2 Tbsp xylitol (optional)
Zest of 1 lime and juice of ½ lime
2 Tbsp coconut flour, almond flour or macadamia flour
2 slightly heaped Tbsp cocoa powder
4 eggs, separarted
Pinch each cream of tartar and salt

Preheat the oven to 180 °C. Grease four ramekins of 8 cm in diameter with the 1 Tbsp butter. Dust with the 1 Tbsp cocoa powder.

In a double boiler or a heatproof bowl suspended above a saucepan of simmering water on medium to high heat, add the chocolate, butter, cream, xylitol, lime zest, juice, coconut flour and cocoa.

In a separate mixing bowl, whisk the egg whites, cream of tartar and salt with an electric mixer until stiff peaks appear. Set aside.

Remove the chocolate mix from the heat and add the egg yolks, one at a time, and whisk in well after each addition. Fold the egg whites into the chocolate mixture. Pour the batter into the ramekins. Bake for 14–15 minures or until firm and a few cracks appear in the surface. Serve immediately with Quick Crème Anglaise (p. 187).

Yields 4 portions

Lemon meringue squares

RECIPE	PORTIONS	TOTAL CARBS	FIBRE	NET CARBS	FAT	PROTEIN	KJ
LM squares	1 block	2.6 g	1.2 g	1.4 g	9.5 g	2.9 g	416

1 quantity Dough 6, Sweet Pie Crust (p. 24)
1 quantity Lemon Custard Filling (p. 169)
1 quantity Royal Icing (p. 157)

Preheat the oven to 180 °C. Line a rectangular 20 cm x 30 cm pan or ovenproof dish with baking paper.

Prepare the pie crust batter, filling and icing as described in the recipes. Press and compact the pie crust in the prepared pan. Bake for 15 minutes or until golden brown. Allow to cool slightly before pouring in a layer of the slightly cooled lemon custard. Refrigerate for 1 hour until the custard is firmly set.

Spread a liberal layer of royal icing on top of the custard. Lift the baking paper out of the pan and cut into 24 squares measuring 5 cm x 5 cm. Use a spatula to lift the squares from the baking paper. Store in an airtight container.

Yields 24 squares

Strawberry crumble squares

RECIPE	PORTIONS	TOTAL CARBS	FIBRE	NET CARBS	FAT	PROTEIN	KJ
Crumble squares	1 block	3.6 g	1.6 g	2 g	7.8 g	1.8 g	348

1 quantity Dough 6, Sweet Pie Crust (p. 24)

STRAWBERRY LAYER
500 g frozen strawberries
2 Tbsp xylitol

Preheat the oven to 180 °C. Line a deep square brownie pan with baking paper.

Prepare the pie crust dough as described in the recipe.

Place the frozen strawberries and xylitol in a heavy-bottomed saucepan on medium heat and simmer gently for 15–20 minutes until reduced to a thicker, jam-like consistency. Allow to cool.

Press and compact half of the crust into the prepared pan. Bake for 15 minutes or until golden brown. Allow to cool slightly before pouring in a layer of the strawberry jam.

Grate the other half of the dough over the strawberry layer to form the crumble topping. Bake for 10 minutes until the crumb layer is golden brown. Allow to cool and then lift the baking paper out of the pan and cut into 16 squares. Use a spatula to lift the squares from the baking paper. Store in an airtight container.

Yields 16 squares

Espresso popsicles

RECIPE	PORTIONS	TOTAL CARBS	FIBRE	NET CARBS	FAT	PROTEIN	KJ
Espresso popsicles	1 popsicle	6.8 g	0 g	6.8 g	6.6 g	2.9 g	396

1 Tbsp gelatine powder
3 Tbsp cool water
¼ cup espresso concentrate (2 shots Nespresso) or ¼ cup boiling water + 2 Tbsp strong instant coffee
2 Tbsp xylitol
1 cup fresh cream or coconut cream
½ cup milk or water
¼ cup amasi
1 tsp vanilla extract
1 Tbsp butter
40 g dark chocolate, chopped

Combine the gelatine and 3 Tbsp water in a small bowl and allow to bloom for a few minutes. Make the boiling hot coffee extract and mix the bloomed gelatine and xylitol into the hot coffee. Stir until dissolved.

Place all the ingredients, except the chocolate, in a blender and blend for 30 seconds. Add the chopped chocolate to the popsicle moulds and gently pour in the espresso cream. Freeze immediately.

Yields 6–8 popsicles

> ### LEKKER TIP
> Melt the chocolate with 2–3 Tbsp coconut oil in a double boiler and then dip the end of the frozen popsicles into the melted chocolate. Place on a baking paper-lined tray in the freezer to set completely.

Koeksisters

THIS IS OFFICIALLY THE SWEETEST RECIPE I HAVE EVER MADE! AND I MADE IT TO ABOUT A THIRD OF THE RECOMMENDED SWEETNESS. I WOULD NOT SUGGEST THIS AS A WEEKLY TREAT, BUT IT DOES MAKE FOR A WONDERFUL WAY TO CELEBRATE AND SHOULD NOT CAUSE A SUGAR SPIKE. I LITERALLY TESTED MY SUGAR LEVELS AFTER TESTING THE RECIPE TWICE.

RECIPE	PORTIONS	TOTAL CARBS	FIBRE	NET CARBS	FAT	PROTEIN	KJ
Koeksisters	1 koeksister	1.9 g	1.2 g	0.7 g	7.1 g	1 g	336

1 quantity Dough 3 (p. 18), made with sunflower seed flour for the right consistency and chilled
1 cup coconut oil for shallow frying

SYRUP
2 cups xylitol
1½ cups water
8 tsp lemon juice
Zest of 1 medium lemon
¼ tsp ground cinnamon
¼ tsp ground ginger
A little less than a ¼ tsp cream of tartar dissolved in 1 Tbsp water

Prepare the dough as described in the recipe.

For the syrup, place all the ingredients into a heavy-bottomed saucepan on medium-high heat and stir until the xylitol has dissolved. Cover and boil for 1 minute. Remove the lid and boil for a further 5 minutes. Do not stir.

Remove from heat and allow to cool completely, then refrigerate for a few hours.

Take the chilled dough ball and roll into golf ball-sized balls (a rope weave works better than a plait for this dough). On a plastic wrap-covered surface, roll the balls into pinky finger-thick laces. Hold the ends together and gently twist into ropes. Pinch the ends together.

Heat the coconut oil in a frying pan on medium to high heat and fry the koeksisters for about 3 minutes on each side or until crispy and golden brown.

Immediately dip the koeksisters into the cold syrup and place on a wire rack to allow the excess syrup to drip off.

Yields 30 medium koeksisters

Monkey bread

A FUN, CROWD-PLEASING DESSERT FOR ALL THE LITTLE AND NOT-SO-LITTLE RASCALS IN YOUR CLAN.

RECIPE	PORTIONS	TOTAL CARBS	FIBRE	NET CARBS	FAT	PROTEIN	KJ
Monkey bread	1 ball	3.4 g	2.2 g	1.2 g	7.3 g	1.6 g	320

2 quantities Dough 3 (p. 18) (nut flour is recommended, but a mix will work too)

SAUCE
6 Tbsp butter
3–4 Tbsp xylitol
1 cup fresh cream

COATING
¼ cup ground cinnamon
2 Tbsp xylitol

Preheat the oven to 180 °C. Grease a Bundt pan. Prepare the dough as described in the recipe.

For the sauce, melt the butter in a saucepan on medium heat, add the xylitol and stir with a whisk until dissolved. Slowly add the cream. Let it simmer and bubble for 5–6 minutes while whisking continuously. Remove from heat.

Mix the coating ingredients together in a small mixing bowl.

Take the chilled dough ball and pinch off pieces of dough. Roll into ping pong-sized balls. Coat and roll each dough ball in the cinnamon-xylitol mixture and pack together tightly in the prepared Bundt pan. Continue until you have filled the Bundt pan with tasty little cinnamon balls. Pour the sauce over the monkey bread and bake for 35–45 minutes or until the sauce is a sticky caramel and the dough balls are firm and spongy.

Allow to cool and set for 5–10 minutes before tipping out onto a serving plate. Serve with a small bowl of Vanilla Icing (p. 146) in the centre of the bread ring.

Yields about 40–45 balls

Apple upside-down puds

RECIPE	PORTIONS	TOTAL CARBS	FIBRE	NET CARBS	FAT	PROTEIN	KJ
Apple puds	1 pudding	6.7 g	2.6 g	4.1 g	16.3 g	5.4 g	744
Apricot puds	1 pudding	5.6 g	2.4 g	3.2 g	16.4 g	5.5 g	728
Banana puds	1 pudding	6.9 g	2.5 g	4.4 g	16.3 g	5.5 g	748

UPSIDE-DOWN TOPPING
1 tsp butter
1 tsp xylitol
Ground cinnamon for sprinkling
1 medium apple, thinly sliced
(you can also use 6 small apricots,
halved, or 36 thin slices banana)

PUDDINGS
2 cups nut flour (I used macadamia)
¼ cup fine desiccated coconut
3 Tbsp xylitol
1 Tbsp baking powder
4 eggs
¼ cup fresh cream
6 Tbsp melted butter
1 tsp vanilla extract

Preheat the oven to 180 °C. Grease a 12-hole regular muffin pan.

Start with the topping. Arrange the butter, xylitol, a generous sprinkling of cinnamon and fruit of your choice in the muffin cups. Pop into the oven for 3–4 minutes to melt and caramelise.

Place the flour, coconut, xylitol and baking powder in a mixing bowl. In a separate bowl, whisk all the remaining ingredients together. Add the wet ingredients to the dry ingredients and mix well. Scoop the batter on top of the fruity layer and bake for 12–15 minutes or until browned and spongy. Serve with the dollop of fresh cream or Quick Crème Anglaise (below).

Yields 12 puddings

Quick Crème Anglaise

RECIPE	PORTIONS	TOTAL CARBS	FIBRE	NET CARBS	FAT	PROTEIN	KJ
Crème anglaise	1	2.5 g	0 g	2.5 g	6.7 g	2.5 g	328

1 tsp vanilla extract
1 cup fresh cream or coconut
cream
3 large egg yolks
2 Tbsp xylitol or sweetener of
choice

Place the vanilla extract and cream in a small heavy-bottomed saucepan and bring to a simmer. Remove from heat.

Whisk the egg yolks and xylitol together in a mixing bowl. Gradually whisk the hot cream mixture into the yolk mixture. Return the custard to the saucepan. Stir over low heat for 4–5 minutes until the custard thickens and leaves a path on the back of the spoon when a finger is drawn across it – do not boil. Strain the sauce into a pouring jug, and then cover and chill.

Yields 1 cup of custard or enough for pouring over 4 puddings

Rustic berry crostata

THIS IS SUCH AN EASY, FRAGRANT AND UNPRETENTIOUS DESSERT, AND IS PERFECT FOR A LARGE DINNER PARTY.
DELICIOUS SERVED COLD WITH A DOLLOP OF WHIPPED CREAM IN SUMMER OR PIPING HOT IN WINTER.

RECIPE	PORTIONS	TOTAL CARBS	FIBRE	NET CARBS	FAT	PROTEIN	KJ
Berry crostata	1	10.6 g	4.7 g	5.9 g	8.9 g	2.7 g	484

1 quantity Dough 2 (p. 17), made
with 2 cups nut flour or 1 nut flour
+ 1 cup sunflower seed flour
Add to the flour mix: ½ tsp salt,
½ tsp mixed spice, 2 Tbsp xylitol
and 1 tsp vanilla extract

BERRY COMPOTE
1 kg mixed frozen berries or 900 g
frozen strawberries and 100 g
blueberries
2 Tbsp xylitol
1 tsp lavender flowers from about
2 English lavender stalks (optional)
1 Tbsp butter, at room temperature
1 egg, beaten
1 cup fresh cream, whipped

Prepare the dough as described in the recipe, simply adding the salt, mixed spice, xylitol and vanilla to the flour of your choice. Refrigerate the dough while you make the berry compote.

Place 900 g of the frozen berries and 1 tsp of the xylitol into a heavy-bottomed saucepan and allow the berries to simmer for 15–20 minutes on medium heat, until thick and well reduced.

In a coffee grinder, grind the remaining xylitol and lavender flowers into a fine, fragrant icing powder.

Preheat the oven to 190 °C.

Roll out the chilled dough ball into a 5 mm-thick oval or circular shape with the dimensions of your baking sheet. Spread the butter over about two-thirds of the dough, leaving a 5–7 cm strip around the dough without butter and ready to fold over.

Spread the berries over the buttered part of the dough. Now start to fold the uncovered dough edge over the berry centre in a loose manner, allowing folds and pleats. Add the remaining 100 g berries (these are for colour and to provide a rustic texture). Brush the beaten egg over the pastry edges and then sprinkle half of the powdered xylitol mixture over the crostata. Bake for 25–30 minutes until fairly dark brown and toasted. Dust with the remainder of the xylitol mixture just before serving with some whipped cream.

Yields about 15 portions

Pumpkin and pecan streusel squares

RECIPE	PORTIONS	TOTAL CARBS	FIBRE	NET CARBS	FAT	PROTEIN	KJ
Streusel squares	1 block	8.3 g	3.6 g	4.7 g	15 g	4 g	700

CRUST

1 quantity Dough 6, Sweet Pie Crust (p. 24)

STREUSEL

½ cup pecans, roughly chopped
½ cup pecans, finely chopped
½ cup nut flour or sunflower seed flour
¼ cup xylitol
¼ tsp salt
1 heaped tsp ground cinnamon
½ tsp mixed spice
Pinch salt
4 slightly heaped Tbsp butter, at room temperature

PUMPKIN CUSTARD

3 Tbsp cold milk or water
1 Tbsp gelatine powder
1 cup fresh cream or coconut cream
6 egg yolks
3 Tbsp xylitol
1½ cups cooked, drained and mashed pumpkin
1½ tsp vanilla extract
1 Tbsp ground cinnamon

For the crust, preheat the oven to 180 °C. Prepare the pie crust batter as described in the recipe. Press and compact the crust in a rectangular 20 x 30 cm pan or ovenproof dish lined with baking paper. Bake for 15 minutes or until golden brown.

For the streusel, gently mix all the ingredients together with your hands. You want a crumb-like or lumpy consistency. Sprinkle the lumps and clusters onto a baking sheet lined with baking paper and bake for 10 minutes.

For the pumpkin custard, combine the milk and gelatine in a small bowl and allow to bloom for a few minutes.

Slowly heat the cream in a medium saucepan until just warm, not boiling.

In a separate mixing bowl, whisk the egg yolks and xylitol. Whisk the lukewarm cream into the egg mixture and pour back into the saucepan. Now, on low heat, stir the custard with a wooden spoon and add the pumpkin, vanilla and cinnamon. Stir for a good few minutes until the custard thickens to a pouring consistency.

Remove from heat, whisk in the gelatine and allow the custard to cool a bit before pouring into the crust. Cool to room temperature, then sprinkle the baked streusel lumps over the slightly cooled custard and refrigerate until set. (You want the custard to be firm enough for the streusel crumbs to sit mostly on top of the custard layer, only sinking into the custard layer ever so slightly.)

Lift the baking paper out of the pan and cut into 24 squares measuring 5 cm x 5 cm. Use a spatula to lift the squares from the baking paper. Store in an airtight container.

Yields 24 squares

Ten-minute cupcakes

RECIPE	PORTIONS	TOTAL CARBS	FIBRE	NET CARBS	FAT	PROTEIN	KJ
Cupcakes	1 cupcake	4.7 g	1.4 g	3.3 g	10.4 g	3.3 g	472

1¼ cups ground pumpkin seeds or ground sunflower seeds (I grind mine in my coffee grinder for about 1 minute; you can substitute with any nut flour too)

3 Tbsp cocoa powder

1 Tbsp baking powder

¼ cup xylitol

½ cup fine desiccated coconut

1 x 35 g bar dark chocolate (85% cocoa solids), chopped (completely optional – I would only suggest this if you plan to eat them dry, as a muffin instead of a cupcake)

½ cup nut meal (I used almond)

4 eggs

1 tsp vanilla extract

⅓ cup melted butter

½ cup fresh cream

QUICK MOCHA ICING

¼ cup cream cheese, at room temperature

¼ cup powdered xylitol (ground in a coffee grinder)

1 tsp instant coffee granules mixed in 1 Tbsp warm water

3 Tbsp cocoa powder

½ cup fresh cream

Mix the ground pumpkin seeds, cocoa, baking powder, xylitol, coconut, dark chocolate chunks and nut meal together in a mixing bowl. In a separate bowl whisk the eggs, vanilla, melted butter and cream together. Pour the wet ingredients into the dry ingredients and mix well.

Scoop into small, medium or large silicone muffin cups, or a lined cupcake pan if you want to bake them in the oven.

In the microwave: Simply bake them in batches of three or four (depending on size) for 2–3 minutes on high setting. The cupcakes should be just set but not dried out so keep an eye on them and check after 2 minutes.

In the oven: Bake at 180 °C for 12–16 minutes. Do a knife test to see if they are baked through, but be sure to take them out while still fairly moist and spongy on top.

For the icing, use an electric mixer to mix all the ingredients together until light and airy with soft peaks. Ice the cupcakes once they are completely cool. This icing has a light mousse-like consistency and can be piped on to make pretty swirls.

Yields 16–18 standard-size cupcakes

Super food beverages and sport snacks

GREEN SMOOTHIES

LET ME INTRODUCE YOU TO YOUR NEW HIGH-FIBRE, PROBIOTIC, CLEANSING, IMMUNE-BOOSTING, HORMONE-HELPING, NUTRIENT-DENSE, METABOLISM-KICKSTARTING, FAT-BURNING SUPER TEAM.

Please note that these are not fat shakes per se, even though they are filled with healthy fats like avocado and chia seeds. They are, however, meant to be (soluble and insoluble) fibre boosters.

THE METHOD BEHIND THE 'SO-CALLED' MADNESS

We need more or less 40 g of fibre per day and you will be shocked to see how little you consume when not intentionally aiming to meet this requirement. No wonder we have clogged up, slowing metabolisms and angry hormones all around. Fibre serves as one of our most important ways to detox on a daily basis and non-starchy veggies are an important part of achieving this as they high in fibre and packed with nutrients.

You will note that I don't have too many recipes containing spinach, kale and non-starchy greens even though I really aim to consume at least eight cups of non-starchy veggies a day. In order to get the required amount of fibre into my diet, I have found that drinking my veggies:
a) makes it a lot easier to consume more of them;
b) saves me a lot of time; and
c) means I benefit from the nutrients in the best possible way as I consume them in their raw form.

I try to have a green smoothie and a salad or two each day, and I apply this same principle to my kids. The secret is to incorporate healthy proteins and fats without too much dairy in your smoothies. We tend to think of smoothies as a fruity version of a milkshake. Now you need to think of your smoothie as super-concentrated nutrients in a manageable serving size. The bottom line is that it does not have to take three bananas, a whole mango and a glass of milk to make a good smoothie. Just the thought of something that sweet makes my blood sugar spike. Bring on the non-starchies!

THE PLAYERS

Choose your super food role players. You get to pick your own team each day. Choose one from each category, or two from the non-starchy greens (always wash your veggies properly). Two green smoothie examples are given on p. 195 to get you started.

Remember that these are not meant to be de-carbed milkshakes. These are nutrient-dense, smart carb ways to boost fibre, metabolism and the immune system, as well as fight inflammation, detox and build a healthy gut environment. They will fill you up with healthy fats while healing your body and lowering your natural weight loss set point.

HEALTHY FATS

Chia seeds (ground)	1 Tbsp
Flax seeds (ground)	1–2 Tbsp
Avocado	¼ fruit
Coconut (fresh, flakes or desiccated)	2 Tbsp
Coconut oil	1 Tbsp
Melted butter	1 Tbsp
Nuts and seeds	1–2 Tbsp

PROBIOTICS (GOOD BUGS FOR THE TUMMY)

Amasi	¼ cup (1 g carbs)
Double-cream plain yoghurt	¼ cup (3 g carbs)
Frozen green peas	¼ cup (3 g carbs)
Dairy-free kefir	¼ cup (3 g carbs)

> ### LEKKER TIP
> Fill an airtight, multi-compartment container with enough chopped veggies, seeds, healthy fats and lower carb fruits in season to make smoothies, salads and snack boxes for the week. It will speed things up on crazy mornings.

PREBIOTICS (GOOD FOOD FOR THE GOOD BUGS IN THE TUMMY)

Asparagus	2–3 spears (you will not taste these in your smoothie at all – unlike leek, onion or garlic, which are also great prebiotic sources)
Fairly unripe banana	¼ (resistant starch with mostly complex carbs; only if you can handle slightly higher amounts of carbs and asparagus is not in season)

PROTEINS

Natural organic whey	20 g
Chia seeds (ground)	2 Tbsp
Hemp powder	15 g
Kale	2 cups (8 g protein)
Eggs (raw)	1 (6 g protein)
Egg whites	3
Nuts and seeds	(2–3 Tbsp)
Nori (torn)	½ sheet

LIQUID BASE

Green tea concentrate (4 green tea bags in 1 cup boiling water – allow to steep and cool)	½–1 cup
Rooibos tea concentrate (1 ginger tea bag and 2 rooibos tea bags in ½ cup boiling water – allow to steep and cool)	½– 1 cup
Chai tea	½–1 cup
Any herbal-based flavoured tea of choice	½–1 cup
Home-made nut or seed milk	½ cup
Coconut milk	¼ cup
Fresh cream	¼ cup
Water	¼–1 cup

LOW-CARB, HIGH-FIBRE GREENS

(choose one or two of these; 1 serving = 1 cup loosely packed leaves)
Spinach
Kale
Broccoli
Beet greens
Turnip greens
Swiss chard
Broccoli leaves
Coriander leaves
Parsley
Dark lettuce
Bok choy
Nori (torn)

FRUITS AND VEGETABLES

Raspberries	¼–½ cup
Blackberries	¼–½ cup
Gooseberries	¼–½ cup
Blueberries	¼–½ cup
Strawberries	¼–½ cup
Hubbard squash	¼–½ cup
Avocado	¼ fruit
Tomatoes	¼–½ cup
Celery	¼–½ cup
Frozen peas	¼ cup
Cucumber	¼–½ cup

HEALTH-BOOSTING FLAVOUR PALETTE
(Warning: Combinations of this category can lead to some highly recommended taste adventures!)
Mixed spice (ground)
Vanilla extract
Coffee powder or espresso shot
Cocoa powder
Turmeric
Cinnamon (ground)
Mint (fresh) or mint oil
Lemon or lime juice
Ginger
Chilli flakes
Cayenne pepper
Black pepper
Himalayan salt

OPTIONAL SWEETENERS
Xylitol
Stevia
Erythritol

Ice (optional)

Example 1: Basic Green Queen

RECIPE	PORTIONS	TOTAL CARBS	FIBRE	NET CARBS	FAT	PROTEIN	KJ
Basic green queen	1	14 g	6.5 g	7.5 g	14.3 g	4.6 g	784

1 cup green tea concentrate (see opposite)
½ cup frozen strawberries
½ cup ice cubes
¼ avocado
1 cup baby spinach
1 cup kale, hard stems removed
2 asparagus spears
2 Tbsp nuts or seeds of choice
¼ sheet nori, torn
¼ cup amasi, double-cream plain yoghurt or coconut cream
Knife point stevia powder or 1 Tbsp xylitol or erythritol

Place all the ingredients together in a blender and blend until creamy and frothy.

Yields 2 portions

Example 2: Royal Blush

RECIPE	PORTIONS	TOTAL CARBS	FIBRE	NET CARBS	FAT	PROTEIN	KJ
Royal blush	1	17.7 g	9.5 g	8.2 g	13 g	16 g	1 564

1 cup rooibos tea concentrate (see opposite)
¼ cup frozen green peas
½ cup ice cubes
½ cup raspberries
1 cup Asian or other lettuce mix
1 cup beet leaves
1 Tbsp chia seeds
1x 20 g scoop pure organic whey
¼ cup amasi, double-cream plain yoghurt or coconut cream
Knifepoint stevia powder or 1 Tbsp xylitol or erythritol
1 tsp vanilla extract

Place all the ingredients together in a blender and blend until creamy.

Yields 2 portions

Better than banana – protein smoothie

RECIPE	PORTIONS	TOTAL CARBS	FIBRE	NET CARBS	FAT	PROTEIN	KJ
Protein smoothie	1	14.5 g	4.3 g	10.2 g	42 g	25.5 g	2 060

2 heaped Tbsp cooked, drained
and mashed pumpkin
¼ tsp ground cinnamon
1 tsp xylitol
1 Tbsp butter, soft or melted
1 cup rooibos tea concentrate
(p. 194)
½ cup coconut cream (or ¼ cup
coconut cream and ¼ cup fresh
cream)
1 x 20 g scoop protein powder
4–6 ice cubes

Place all the ingredients in a blender and blend for a minute or so. Serve over crushed ice or drink as is. This smoothie is a great low-carb meal in a glass.

Yields 1 portion

HOME-MADE DAIRY-FREE MILK ALTERNATIVES

Flax milk

RECIPE	PORTIONS	TOTAL CARBS	FIBRE	NET CARBS	FAT	PROTEIN	KJ
Flax milk	1	3 g	0 g	3 g	2.9 g	1.7 g	212

⅓ cup flax seeds
2½ cups water (plus 1½ cups to
add later for desired consistency)
1 Tbsp xylitol or ¼ tsp stevia, or
simply to taste
1 tsp vanilla extract
½ tsp ground cinnamon
¼ tsp salt

Combine the flax seeds and 2½ cups water in a blender and blend for at least 1 minute until thick and creamy. Pour the thick milk through cheesecloth to strain out the seed shells.

Once strained, add the xylitol, vanilla, cinnamon and salt, plus more water to achieve the desired consistency.

Serve right away or chill for later use.

Yields just over 1 litre (4 portions)

Coconut milk

RECIPE	PORTIONS	TOTAL CARBS	FIBRE	NET CARBS	FAT	PROTEIN	KJ
Coconut milk	1	5 g	0 g	5 g	12.9 g	1.4 g	544

1 cup desiccated coconut
3 cups water (plus 1 cup water to add later for desired consistency)
1 Tbsp xylitol or ¼ tsp stevia
1 tsp vanilla extract
½ tsp ground cinnamon
¼ tsp salt

Combine the desiccated coconut and 3 cups water in a blender and blend for at least 1 minute until thick and creamy. Pour the thick milk through cheesecloth to strain out the coconut. Once strained, add the xylitol, vanilla, cinnamon and salt, plus more water to achieve the desired consistency. Serve right away or chill for later use.

Yields just over 1 litre (4 portions)

LEKKER TIPS

- Invest in a few sheets of cheesecloth (available at fabric stores) so that they're always ready at hand.
- Use the same ratios as the coconut milk to make sunflower seed milk or any nut milk of your choosing. Add turmeric, cocoa, espresso, vanilla or berries for a lovely flavoured bevarage.
- All these milks can be stored for 2–3 days in the refrigerator. Rather make a smaller batch and use it all.

Immune booster tea

RECIPE	PORTIONS	TOTAL CARBS	FIBRE	NET CARBS	FAT	PROTEIN	KJ
Booster tea	1	6.4 g	2.5 g	3.9 g	27 g	2.4 g	1 048

6 rooibos or rooibos chai tea bags
1 Tbsp gelatine powder
Xylitol or stevia to taste
1 tsp turmeric
¼ tsp ground ginger or 1 tsp grated fresh ginger
½ tsp ground cinnamon
Pinch each ground cardamom, ground black pepper and salt
1 Tbsp butter or coconut oil
2 cups boiling water
1 x 400 ml can coconut milk or any Home-made Dairy-free Milk Alternative (pp. 196–197)

In a saucepan, steep the rooibos tea, gelatine, sweetener, spices and butter in the boiling water for 5–10 minutes. Remove the tea bags and add the coconut milk. Reheat on the stove and serve warm or blend half of the slightly cooled mixture at a time to emulsify the fats. This makes for a divine frothy drink.

Yields 3–4 cups of golden awesomeness

ENERGY DRINKS – LOW-CARB STYLE

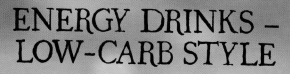

CHIA SEEDS AND GREEN TEA ARE BOTH EXCELLENT ENERGY BOOSTERS. CHIA SEEDS ALSO HAVE GREAT ELECTROLYTE-BOOSTING PROPERTIES. ADD ANTIOXIDANT-RICH ROOIBOS TEA AND STAYING HYDRATED AND ENERGISED SUDDENLY TAKES ON A NEW MEANING. WHO NEEDS WINGS IF YOU HAVE A JETPACK?

Mama Mia Chia

RECIPE	PORTIONS	TOTAL CARBS
Mama Mia chia	1	9 g

FIBRE	NET CARBS	FAT	PROTEIN	KJ
5.7 g	3.3 g	9 g	4.9 g	312

1 cup tea concentrate (2 green tea tea bags and
4 rooibos tea bags steeped in 1 cup boiling water)
5–6 fresh or frozen strawberries
1 Tbsp chia seeds
Knife point debittered stevia or 2 tsp xylitol
1 tsp vanilla extract
1 cup ice
1 cup cold water

Place all the ingredients together in a blender and blend until creamy.

This yields two servings for you to use as needed during a run or ride. It is not oily or fatty and does not cause phlegm build-up. I take a half portion to the gym for a hydrating drink between HIIT (high-intensity interval training) sessions.

Yields 1 portion

Chia Blerry Mary

T'IS A DRINK WITH A KICK ... AND ALSO MY FAVOURITE.

RECIPE	PORTIONS	TOTAL CARBS	FIBRE	NET CARBS	FAT	PROTEIN	KJ
Chia Blerry Mary	1	13.5 g	10.8 g	2.7 g	9.3 g	4.9 g	580

1 cup tea concentrate (2 minted green tea tea bags, 1 ginger tea bag or 1 Tbsp grated fresh ginger and 2 Tbsp lemon juice in 1 cup boiling water)
1 Tbsp chia seeds
Knife point debittered stevia or 2 tsp xylitol
1 cup ice
Water as needed

Place all the ingredients together in a blender and blend until creamy.

Yields 1 refreshing portion

> LEKKER TIP
> My husband does strength training and uses these energy drinks as a base to which he adds his natural, unflavoured BCAAs (branched chain amino acids). He also phones me right away if he had a tough session in the gym, usually to hear me confess that I forgot to add the chia seeds.

Ninja Chai Tea

RECIPE	PORTIONS	TOTAL CARBS	FIBRE	NET CARBS	FAT	PROTEIN	KJ
Ninja chai tea	1	3.5 g	1.5 g	2 g	13.6 g	0.5 g	520

2 cups water
4 rooibos or rooibos chai tea bags (Ceylon tea will work too)
1 tsp ground mixed spice
½ tsp ground ginger or a chunk of fresh ginger, peeled
1 cinnamon stick (optional)
4 whole cloves
6 whole cardamom seeds, crushed
1 tsp black peppercorns
1 Tbsp coconut oil
1 Tbsp butter
2 Tbsp fresh cream (you can use a bit more to taste, but this is the only component that will push up the carbs)
Debittered stevia powder (optional)

Combine the water, tea bags and spices in a saucepan and bring to a boil. Keep it on high heat for a few minutes before setting aside and allowing to steep for 5 minutes.

Add the coconut oil, butter and cream to a blender. Use a sieve to strain the spiced tea mixture into the blender. Add a pinch of stevia if you would prefer a sweeter tea. Blend for 1 minute or until all the fats have emulsified and it has a creamy, frothy, rich consistency.

Sprinkle with a bit of extra mixed spice or ground cinnamon.

Yields 2 portions

iFuel squares

RECIPE	PORTIONS	TOTAL CARBS	FIBRE	NET CARBS	FAT	PROTEIN	KJ
iFuel squares	1 square	5.5 g	2 g	3.5 g	17.3 g	9.7 g	848

SQUARES

½ cup melted coconut oil
½ cup coconut cream
1 x 20 g scoop protein powder
1 Tbsp vanilla extract
1 Tbsp ground coffee beans
1 cup desiccated coconut (ground in a coffee grinder)
1 cup nut flour of choice (I prefer macadamia)
½ cup pumpkin seeds (ground in a coffee grinder)
½ cup sunflower seeds (ground in a coffee grinder)
1–2 Tbsp xylitol
2 Tbsp chia seeds (ground in a coffee grinder)

CHOC TOPPING

¼ cup coconut cream
¼ cup cocoa powder
2 Tbsp xylitol
2 Tbsp coconut oil

Put all the squares ingredients into a mixing bowl. Divide into two equal batches and use a blender to mix them into a spreadable batter. Press and compact the batter in a square brownie pan lined with baking paper.

For the topping, stir all the topping ingredients together in a saucepan on medium heat and allow it to thicken into a shiny ganache-like consistency. Spread the topping over the squares layer.

Place in the freezer for 5–10 minutes to set, then take out and cut into 20 squares. Return to the freezer and let it set completely before serving or packing as a post-workout gym snack. (Unfortunately, the bars are not good at withstanding the heat.)

Yields 20 squares

Protein pumpkin muffins

RECIPE	PORTIONS	TOTAL CARBS	FIBRE	NET CARBS	FAT	PROTEIN	KJ
Pumpkin muffins	1 muffin	3.9 g	0.7 g	3.2 g	11.9 g	14.2 g	716

6 eggs
½ cup melted butter
½ cup cooked, drained and mashed pumpkin
1 Tbsp apple cider vinegar
½ cup coconut flour
6 x 20 g scoops protein powder
1–2 Tbsp xylitol or ¼ tsp stevia
1 tsp baking powder
1 tsp ground cinnamon
1 Tbsp vanilla extract
½ tsp salt
Mixed spice for sprinkling

Preheat the oven to 180 °C.

Mix the eggs, melted butter, pumpkin and vinegar together in a mixing bowl. In a separate bowl, mix the flour, protein powder, xylitol, baking powder, ground cinnamon, vanilla and salt together. Pour the wet mixture into the dry mixture, stir well and wait for the dough to firm up a bit. Scoop into a 12-hole regular muffin pan and sprinkle with mixed spice.

Bake for 25–30 minutes until golden. Do the knife test to make sure they are baked through and firm.

Yields 12 muffins

Conversion chart

Metric	US cups
5 ml	1 tsp
15 ml	1 Tbsp
60 ml	4 Tbsp or ¼ cup
80 ml	⅓ cup
125 ml	½ cup
160 ml	⅔ cup
200 ml	¾ cup
250 ml	1 cup

Index

Page numbers in **bold** indicate photographs.